ROLAND N

Department of Mu

SCORES
AND SKETCHES:
AN ANTHOLOGY FOR THE LISTENER

▲▼ ADDISON-WESLEY PUBLISHING COMPANY

Reading, Massachusetts · Menlo Park, California · London · Don Mills, Ontario

The musical scores printed in this text were drawn by Robert Bockholt.

PREFACE

Scores and Sketches: An Anthology for the Listener is a flexible book
which can be used in several pedagogical situations. It can be used in
courses for non-music majors such as Music Appreciation, Music History
Survey, or Fundamentals of Music. The introductory chapter, "How to
Follow a Score Sketch," is designed specifically for the non-music major
who does not read music. There he will learn how to find his way about a
score and keep his place by locating important visual elements. Such
visual cues include the abbreviations indicating various instruments, melodic shapes, and dynamic markings. The non-music major will not need
to identify pitches or rhythmic values. However, the book can be used
equally well in courses for music majors such as History of Music, Form,
Conducting, Harmony, or Counterpoint. The music major, since he probably reads music, will use the scores as a basis for more detailed study
than is expected of the non-music major. Scores and Sketches is thus a
practical text which can find its place in several different classroom situations, including classes where both music majors and non-music majors
are present.

This text contains three basic components:

1. The various kinds of scores: (a) original scores, (b) piano reduc-
    tions, (c) Score Sketches containing the leading melodic lines of an
    entire work or movement, and (d) full orchestral scores with the
    leading melodic lines "grayed out" (shaded) for emphasis.

2. The introductions to the basic periods of music: Renaissance,
    Baroque, Classicism, Romanticism, and the Twentieth Century.
    Though brief, each of these introductions gives a number of impor-
    tant points that will prepare the reader to understand the scores
    that follow.

3. The analyses and questions for discussion. These may be used as
    the basis for classroom discussions, oral or written reports, term
    papers, etc.

Because the book contains stylistic and historical information as
well as several kinds of annotated scores, emphasis can be placed on
either the literary or the theoretical aspects of music. Where the emphasis falls will depend on the conformation of the class and on the pedagogical
aims of the instructor.

We wish to thank Dr. Colleen Bicknell of Northeastern University
for reading and making suggestions about portions of the text. Dr. Martin
Robbins, also of Northeastern University, is responsible for most of the
poetic translations which appear in the text.

The authors hope that the materials included in this text will help bring the listener one step closer to the composer.

Boston, Massachusetts   R. N.

March 1971   W. T.

CONTENTS

HOW TO FOLLOW A SCORE SKETCH

Following music is one thing; reading music is another. Learning to follow
a single-line score sketch is a matter of a few concentrated hours of effort;
reading music fluently and easily requires years of patient application.

When you read music, say at the piano, you must instantly decipher
multiple musical symbols at a given rate of speed. You must hear with
your inner ear the sounds symbolized by the notation, and then locate these
sounds on the keyboard with fingers strong and agile enough to meet the
technical requirements of the composition. This is a formidable task,
especially when you are reading at first sight. Sight reading on any other
instrument, or with the voice, or even silently, presents comparable
difficulties.

However, when you follow the music in this book, your purpose is
not to produce music yourself — though ultimately you may wish to do so.
Rather it is to enhance your understanding and enjoyment of music by
becoming familiar with the visual analog of your aural experience. You
will see what the composer wrote, what the musician reads. Then, by
your observation of the salient points of the composition as represented by
the Score Sketch, you will learn how to listen at a deeper level. You will
see and understand structure, texture, and the performance forces represented on the Score Sketch. By study and repeated looking/listening you
will come to feel and know the music in its wholeness — well defined,
emotionally satisfying, and unique.

1. How to Start Examining the Score Sketch

Begin with a sketch on a single staff. The skill that you acquire by studying
this kind of sketch can easily be applied to sketches with multiple staves.
Work with only one piece, movement, or part at a time. Know who the
composer is, what kind of structure is involved, what the performance
medium is. The page immediately facing each Score Sketch in this book
will give you this preliminary information.

Before listening to a recording, examine the Score Sketch throughout. Look for all non-notational signs and words pertaining to the performance of the music. You will find directions and signs for tempo, dynamics, articulation, repeats, instrumental or vocal forces, etc. If you do not
already know what these mean, look them up in a music dictionary or com-
prehensive music appreciation text. Write on the Score Sketch the meaning
of terms that you are not already familiar with. It is especially important
that you understand the tempo indication at the beginning of the Score
Sketch. This is placed immediately above the first measure. It suggests
how fast your eye will have to move from note to note or measure to
measure. Watch for possible changes of tempo later on.

Find the time signature. It immediately follows the key signature
at the beginning of the first measure. The upper number gives you the
number of counts (beats) in each measure. If the upper number is 6, 9, or
12 and the tempo is moderate or fast, divide the upper number by 3. The

resulting number will indicate the actual counts in each measure. If the sign is C, count four; if it is $\math022{C}$, count two.

2. Listening for Pulse and Tempo

Now listen to the recording, without looking at the Score Sketch. Get the feeling of the pulse rate. Tap each pulse with your hand at the correct tempo. Listen very carefully for fluctuations of tempo (rubato). For purposes of phrasing and interpretation the tempo will sometimes slacken or move ahead temporarily.

As you tap each pulse at the correct tempo, count to yourself the number of beats indicated by the time signature. If you listen carefully you will feel that very often one of the pulses receives more stress than the others. Usually this will be the first count. Count "one" for each stressed pulse and follow through in each measure while you tap.

3. Putting It Together

Return to the Score Sketch. This time listen while you follow. Again count the correct number of beats for each measure at the correct tempo. But now, each time that you say "one," place your finger below and immediately to the right of each successive bar line. Continue to the end. Do this several times. Eventually you will be able to dispense with counting. Once you have acquired the ability to keep your place in the sketch, you will have found the means for considerable enhancement of your musical enjoyment and understanding.

4. Listening in Depth

You may now examine the music in depth for structure, melodic contour, instrumental or vocal combinations, rhythmic features, etc. If the Score Sketch consists of multiple staves, you will want to follow each one separately to the end, or perhaps skip from one to the other. Experiment constantly. Try to hear more and more each time. While following a single-staff Score Sketch listen for elements not represented. Try to imagine what they would look like in notation. When you get to the full orchestral scores in the book, follow each individual staff through to the end, noting the unique role of the instrument involved. Then try to follow all the instruments of each choir, then the full score. Once you have acquired this ability you will have a solid concept of the harmonic depth of music as well as its melodic direction. This is an achievement well within the grasp of the serious listener.

". . . there is serious reason for protesting against the neglect of score-reading in the training, not only of professional musicians, but of all music lovers."

> Sir Donald Francis Tovey
> (from The Training of the
> Musical Imagination)

PART I THE RENAISSANCE

The intrinsic nature of the Renaissance as a rebirth of the arts — a new exploration of the ideals of classical antiquity — was parallel to the new recognition of the importance of the individual. In music this period was not so much a "renaissance" (a term borrowed from the other arts, anyway) as it was a burgeoning. The result was a musical style that did not break its links with the past but nevertheless reached out to embrace a more personal expression than was ever exhibited before. This attitude of "self" is the hallmark of the Renaissance.

The Renaissance man was aware of the importance of the individual's personal contribution as opposed to the primacy of tradition. Dante had already introduced the expression l'uomo universale. "Universal man" — or "all-sided man" in Jacob Burkhardt's terminology — expresses the ideal of the Renaissance man: the fullest possible realization of self. The personal dynamism that was to be characteristic of Renaissance man was expressed by Leon Battista Alberti (c. 1404-1472): "Men can do all things if they will."

The Renaissance period in music (1450-1600) is commonly referred to as "the golden age of vocal polyphony." This phrase does indeed characterize the period, especially at its height, but it should not lead us to ignore the gradually increasing use of instruments: in solos, in consort, or together with voices. The lute had long been in use, serving since the time of the troubadours and the jongleurs of the twelfth century as a solo instrument or accompanying instrument. The organ, of course, was a fixture in cathedrals and chapels. Brass instruments were used to add a brilliance to festive occasions; a set of recorders of various sizes was more appropriate for intimate musical gatherings. The consort of viols was well established in the late Renaissance and for a cultured family it was almost de rigueur to have a bank of viols. The virginal and like instruments were popular keyboard instruments in the home.

In the Renaissance it was common practice for many of these instruments to either double or take the place of voice parts. Ensemble forces were most flexible and heterogeneous.

In the middle of the fifteenth century, music had traveled the long distance from the monophony of Gregorian chant to a polyphony that included very complex uses of contrapuntal devices. The first break from monophony had occurred sometime before the tenth century, with organum: two voices in parallel 4ths or 5ths. Thereafter in two-part writing the lines gradually became more independent. By the twelfth century there was enough distinction (both melodic and rhythmic) between the voices so that one can speak of polyphony. The plainsong of the Gregorian chant in the lower voice, referred to as the cantus firmus, was now coupled with a weaving florid line in the upper.

Widening of the musical fabric to include additional strands occurred in the twelfth and thirteenth centuries. The thirteenth-century motet was an important development, and included the macaronic combina-

3

tion of texts (texts in different languages, one of which was usually Latin).
The thirteenth century saw other developments as well, such as the conduc-
tus, with the lower (tenor) part newly composed rather than taken from
plainsong. In the fourteenth century a new unifying device, isorhythm,
was established; isorhythm involves the repetition of rhythmic patterns.
Until the fifteenth century the cantus firmus, whether based on plainsong
or other material, had always been restricted to the lowest voice. But at
this time another voice was put below the tenor and thus were established
the now basic four parts of choral writing: soprano, alto, tenor, and bass.

Beginning about the middle of the fifteenth century the Netherlands
became the focal point from which emanated some of the most important
developments in the music of the Renaissance. These developments would
ultimately touch all of the important composers of the Renaissance.

One of the most influential of these composers was Johannes
Ockeghem (c. 1420-1495), who was to influence a whole generation of composers with his concepts of melodic continuity, animation, and cohesion
between the voices. The following generation of composers born about the
middle of the fifteenth century included Jacob Obrecht (c. 1452-1505),
Heinrich Isaac (c. 1450-1517), and Josquin des Prez (c. 1440-1521). It
was Josquin who was to become the first outstanding musical figure of the
Renaissance.

Josquin, born in the Netherlands but international in his influence,
was to plant the seeds that would ultimately come to full flower nearly a
century later in the music of a later Netherlander, Orlandus Lassus.
Josquin studied with Ockeghem and from him thoroughly learned all the
devices and complexities of past styles and techniques; more important,
however, he was strongly influenced by Ockeghem's personal approach to
the handling of polyphonic sonority.

Josquin is the Janus figure of his time. His music embodies the
older uses of modality, but at the same time reaches toward tonality. Out
of the contrapuntal web rises a sense of melody for its own sake. And
combined with the manipulations of canon there is a striving for purely
esthetic effects as well.

Josquin, in the difficult role of transition figure, sought to make a
personal expression far different from any that had appeared before. In
the Renaissance fashion he hewed out of the immediate past a style and a
manner more representative of the individual than had heretofore been
known. Before Josquin the idea of imitation among the parts had at times
been carried to the point of absurdity, with composers vying to outdo one
another in what might be called a game of musical mathematics. In some
instances technique had become the sole justification for a composition.
Technique, always the first necessity, cannot by itself fulfill the total
obligation of a composer.

The most important forms to develop in the sixteenth century were
the mass, the motet, and the chanson. Josquin contributed notably to the
literature of each of these. The composers who followed Josquin contributed in various ways to the gradually enlarging corpus of the polyphonic
style.

Two other Netherlands composers of importance followed Josquin.
Nicolas Gombert (c. 1490-1556), who may have been a pupil of Josquin,
was not as personal or dramatic in his musical expression but nevertheless

carried forward Josquin's efforts in the area of sensitivity to texts.
Jacobus Clemens (c. 1510-1556), although sometimes writing in a style
similar to Gombert's, was in certain works more intense and dramatic.
     The practice of musica ficta during this period became more and
more marked. This practice, in which the performer chromatically
altered tones not specifically marked for such alteration, probably origi-
nated for melodic reasons.
     The Netherlands style was continued by Adrian Willaert (c. 1490-
1562). As director of music — conductor, composer, and teacher — at
St. Mark's Cathedral in Venice, his influence spread throughout Italy. He
was one of the leaders in establishing the Venetian school of composition
which later was to include the Gabrielis, Andrea (c. 1510-1586) and his
nephew Giovanni (c. 1557-1612).
     The last important development in Renaissance vocal polyphony was
the madrigal. Early in the sixteenth century, secular music had been
flourishing. Of the various songs and dances of the street the frottola
emerged to become an important part of the evolutionary process that led
to the sixteenth-century madrigal. The frottola had been in vogue since
about 1500, and consisted of several stanzas preceded by a refrain which
was also repeated at the end.
     The poets of the period had revived the name madrigal from the
poetic form popular in the fourteenth century. The earlier madrigal was
pastoral, or even rustic, in origin, but the sixteenth-century madrigal was
a highly sophisticated musical setting of richly expressive poetry.
     The secular lightheartedness of the frottola was carried over into
the early madrigals, especially in the choice of text. The music of the
madrigal at first was similar to that of the frottola in its use of three or
four voices in an essentially homophonic manner, with one voice standing
out as the melody.
     The leading composers of the early period of madrigal writing were
Costanza Festa (c. 1480-1540) of Rome, and Jacob Arcadelt (c. 1505-c.
1560). Word-painting at this time was naively explicit, but it was to lead
to the implicit word-painting of the great composers of the latter part of
the century. The inner subtleties of meaning in the text became the well-
spring for the evocation of mood through music.
     In the last half of the century we find a powerful musical personality
in Luca Marenzio (1553-1599). In his canonic style, his feeling for the
proportions of polyphony and homophony, his chromaticism, his detailed
word-painting, he is representative of the ideal style of the late sixteenth-
century Italian madrigal. It was at this time that the madrigal passed to
England, chiefly through a collection titled Musica Transalpina. In it were
included works by Marenzio, de Rore, and other Italian madrigalists. This
collection, the first with English words, was published in London in 1588.
     The Italian madrigal had been known in England some years before
this through manuscript copies, but its influence had not been wide. However, one English composer, William Byrd, had been greatly influenced by
the style and beauty of the Italian madrigal. Two of his madrigals were
included in the Musica Transalpina collection. Thus William Byrd (1543-
1623), along with Thomas Morley (1557-c. 1603), began what was to become one of England's greatest periods of musical achievement. The
English made the madrigal their own, and in the seventeenth century a

great number of madrigals and other vocal works provided an outstanding literature.

There is one other composer who must be mentioned in any discussion of the madrigal. Out of the mainstream and exercising little direct influence, Carlo Gesualdo (1560–1613) carried word-painting to an extreme not previously approached through a chromaticism more daring than that of any of his contemporaries.

But the two composers who best represent the culmination of the Renaissance ideal in music — the equalization of all the voices, with an emotional expression that is entwined with the text — are Orlando di Lasso, sometimes called Orlandus Lassus (1532–1594), a Flemish composer, and Giovanni Pierluigi da Palestrina (c. 1525–1594).

The works of Palestrina, almost all intended for the church, in general exhibit a serenity of style that is considered by some to be the purest expression of the late sixteenth century. It is his work that is often used for studies of sixteenth-century counterpoint. But it is di Lasso who more truly represents the broad spectrum of late sixteenth-century writing. His contributions include not only works for the church (motets, masses, magnificats, passions, psalms) but also secular works (chansons, madrigals, German choral lieder). Because of his broad scope, his broad range of expression, and his place among the international composers, it may be said that what Josquin began in the second half of the fifteenth century came to fruition with di Lasso in the second half of the sixteenth.

In the last half of the sixteenth century there was a renewed interest in church music as a result of both the Reformation and the Counter-Reformation. But once man had turned, even partially, away from the rigid authority of the church, the way was open for new developments in all areas of society and the arts. The spirit of individuality had been renewed. And in music the affirmation of the individual prepared the way for a new expression. Opera was about to be born.

ABSALON, FILI MI

Josquin des Prez (c. 1440–1521)

Of about 100 motets written by Josquin, Absalon, Fili Mi is not only one of
the most beautiful, but it is also among the more advanced in style. Published in the early sixteenth century, this work shows Josquin's freer style,
in which he seeks a beautifully flowing line in each of the parts.
    The following score is in modern notation.

Structure: Motet

Translation:

Absalon, my son,
Who wills that I would die for you!
Absalon, my son,
I live no longer,
but shall descend to hell, weeping.

FOR DISCUSSION

1. Note the entrances of the alto, tenor, and bass in mm. 3, 4, and 6 in imitation of the opening voice.

2. Note the change of effect at m. 56 at which moment the music is suddenly homophonic for $1\frac{1}{2}$ measures. This is the first time in the work that all voices are together at the harmonic cadence. This new section (mm. 56–68) is repeated almost exactly (mm. 73–85) at the close of the work.

3. Beginning at m. 61, note the musical tone-painting suggested by the Latin word descendam. Josquin's response to the text is quite simple and direct: he sets the Latin with imitative descending lines sequenced in all parts. But the musical result is one of great beauty as the voices successively follow each other at the distance of a half-note, each part descending in 3rds. Also note the effect of syncopation in this passage.

4. To what extent does this work foreshadow the later use of major-minor tonality? How much evidence is there of leading-tone tendencies?

5. Compare the melodic contours of Absalon, Fili Mi with those of Et Incarnatus Est from the B Minor Mass of J. S. Bach in Part II of this text. To what extent does the difference between these melodic contours reflect the differing esthetic of the Renaissance and Baroque periods?

FA UNA CANZONE

Orazio Vecchi (1550-1605)

A canzone (and canzonetta, the diminutive form) is a short secular vocal work, quite common in sixteenth-century Italy. Vecchi, born in Modena, in the last years of his life was maestro di cappella at the cathedral in Modena and was also employed by the Duke of Modena.

Well-regarded as a composer in his day, he is known best for his L'Amfiparnasso (The Slopes of Parnassus), a madrigal comedy. Six books of his canzonette were published as well as masses, motets, and other works.

There are no bar lines in the original. There are five verses in the original.

Structure: Canzonetta

Translation (by Dr. Martin Robbins):

Sing a song to me without black notes, *
If e'er you long to have my favor:
Make it of such a tone that invites,
Sweetly coming to its end, slumber.

_____

* A pun on black notes as sorrowful because of their color; this line also implies that the singer should perform the work simply and not sing many ornate runs of black notes. (This, like the tone of the song, is not serious — ornate runs were quite common at this time.)

FOR DISCUSSION

1. Note the ambivalence of tonality caused by the swing of emphasis from
    B flat to G as chord roots. Does this suggest a modal tonality or does
    it look forward to the later major-minor system?

2. Note the varying rhythmic accents symbolized here by the modern use
    of changing time signatures. Compare this with Stravinsky's use of
    meter in L'Histoire du Soldat (Part V of this text).

3. In mm. 11-14 what compositional devices are used — textural, melodic,
    rhythmic — to achieve change of pace and imagery?

IO PUR RESPIRO

Carlo Gesualdo (c. 1560–1613)

Gesualdo, who had a more than ordinary private life, wrote more than ordinary music. (See the biography by Gray and Heseltine, Carlo Gesualdo, Prince of Venosa, Musician and Murderer.) His uses of chromaticism went far beyond the norm of the late sixteenth century. His music embodies an extreme expression of the Renaissance concept of individuality.

His first book of madrigals appeared in 1594, the year in which both di Lasso and Palestrina died.

Io pur respiro illustrates the advanced chromaticism that was a unique part of Gesualdo's style, and illustrates also the intimate connection between words and music.

This madrigal and other examples of Renaissance vocal style may be found in the Historical Anthology of Music by Davison and Apel (published by Harvard University Press, 1954).

Structure: Madrigal

Translation (by Dr. Martin Robbins):

Still I breathe in such a great sorrow,
Still, pitiless heart, I live somehow.
O, there is not much more hope to have
That we again will see our good love.
O, Death, help me
To kill this life;
In pity strike the blow
That ends my life
And all this great sorrow.

FOR DISCUSSION

1. First, quickly scan the madrigal and note its overall architectonic plan.

2. What are the proportions of polyphony and homophony? Note the varying densities of texture.

3. What are the uses of imitation in both diatonic and chromatic style?

4. Consider specific instances of tone-painting:

   a) "I still breathe," mm. 1-4

   b) "Oh, pitiless heart," mm. 19-22

   Find other examples.

5. Consider the different ways in which chromaticism is used. For example, how does the chromaticism of mm. 5-13 differ from that of mm. 19-22? How does the treatment of the words gran dolore near the beginning compare with that for gran duolo near the beginning? What are the possible reasons?

THE CARMAN'S WHISTLE

William Byrd (1543-1623)

"The Carman's Whistle," chosen by Byrd as the basis for a set of variations, was a popular ballad in Elizabethan England. The ballad in the sixteenth century was a narrative song in which the music was repeated for each verse. It often dealt with events of the day, or told a tale, amorous or witty, or both. "The Carman's Whistle" was known at least as early as 1592.

The text is from The Ballad Literature and Popular Music of the Olden Time, by William Chappell (first published in 1859). There are twelve verses in the original, of which the first five are presented here.

2. So comely was her countenance,
    And "winning was her air,"
    As though the goddess Venus
    Herself she had been there;
    And many a smirking smile she gave
    Amongst the leaves so green,
    Although she was perceived,
    She thought she was not seen.

3. At length she chang'd her countenance,
    And sung a mournful song,
    Lamenting her misfortune
    She staid a maid so long;
    Sure young men are hard-hearted,
    And know not what they do,
    Or else they want for compliments
    Fair maidens for to woo.

4. Why should young virgins pine away
    And lose their chiefest prime;
    And all for want of sweet-hearts
    To cheer us up in time?
    The young man heard her ditty,
    And could no longer stay,
    But straight unto the damosel
    With speed he did away.

5. When he had played unto her
    One merry note or two,
    Then was she so rejoiced,
    She knew not what to do:
    O God-a-mercy, carman,
    Though art a lively lad;
    Thou hast as rare a whistle
    As ever carman had.

The carman (or carter), as opposed to the coachman, was considered in some quarters to be able to cheer his horses, when they got tired, with his whistling of a current ballad. The coachman, on the other hand, used oaths for his tired beasts.

Shakespeare, in <u>King Henry IV, Part 2</u>, had Falstaff say this of Justice Shallow: he "came ever in the rearward of the fashion, and sung those tunes to the overscutched huswives that he heard the carmen whistle, and sware they were his fancies or good-nights."

The manuscript of William Byrd's set of variations on this tune is in a collection of virginal music preserved in the Fitzwilliam Museum, Cambridge, England. This collection, long known as <u>Queen Elizabeth's Virginal Book</u>, was printed for the first time in 1889 as <u>The Fitzwilliam Virginal Book</u>.

<u>Structure</u>: Theme and variations

FOR DISCUSSION

1. Compare Byrd's first presentation of the tune with the original folk
    song. Note that Byrd sets the melody an octave lower than the original
    for the first two measures. Note also two other points: the left hand
    waits until m. 2, and then begins canonically in imitation of the tune a
    5th lower; at the same time the melody is changed in the right hand.
    Why is this? You will discover that Byrd has used the first two mea-
    sures as an introduction to the entire work; they do not appear in any
    of the variations. Consider possible reasons for this.

2. The system of measures (and bar lines) in use today was not yet estab-
    lished in Byrd's time. Note Byrd's use of bar lines.

3. Compare each variation with the first presentation and note to what ex-
    tent the melody of each adheres to or departs from the original contour.

4. Note the use of progressive rhythmic animation by the gradual intro-
    duction of quicker notes (shorter note values) through Variation 7. Why
    is this rhythmic animation discontinued at Variation 8?

5. Compare these variations with others in this book: the Finale of
    Mozart's Clarinet Quintet (in Part III); Schubert's Variations on "Death
    and the Maiden" (in Part IV); and Liszt's Totentanz (in Part IV). Of
    the two basic types of variations, ornamental and characteristic, find
    the proportion of each used in these works.

PART II THE BAROQUE

The music of the Baroque period (c. 1600-1750) displays striking contrasts.
Though it is alive and energetic, capable of expressing intense subjective
emotional states, it is also saturated with complex structures suggesting
great intellectual objectivity. The Crucifixus from the B Minor Mass by
J. S. Bach, for example, is as poignant as anything found in the later
Romantic period, but its variation structure (chaconne) is intellectually
most rigorous.

Perhaps these esthetic antinomies explain why the Baroque offers so
much to so many. The amateur player cherishes his Telemann, Handel,
and Bach not only because they seldom require virtuosity, but because they
satisfy emotionally. Through the complex textures he can realize high ensemble values as he joins his part with others in various chamber combinations. The amateur chorister, for similar reasons, derives immense
satisfaction from his voice part no matter what the register: soprano, alto,
tenor, or bass. The professional musician finds in the Baroque the ideal
mix of the rational with the passionate. He can satisfy a craving for analysis but never be sated by its intellectuality. And he can derive emotional
satisfaction from his performance of these works so full of vital energy and
feeling.

The lay listener, though initially the dense textures and elegant
style of the period may seem alien to him, soon learns that the music is
very much alive. The ever-bubbling counterpoint, kept moving by the unflagging beat of the allegro movements, soon captures his fancy. A clear
indication of interest in Baroque music is its recent utilization by several
jazz or jazz-oriented instrumental and vocal groups. The affinity of jazz
to Baroque music (especially in its rhythmic aspects) has been discovered,
explored, and put to wide popular use.

Melody typifies Baroque antinomies. Sometimes Baroque melody
is short and plain, especially at the head of complicated polyphonic structures such as the fugue or the chaconne. For example, the subject of the
Fugue in C Sharp Minor from Book 1 of the Well Tempered Clavier by J. S.
Bach consists of only five notes: C sharp, B sharp, E natural, D sharp,
C sharp. At other times, particularly in the slow pieces, Baroque melody
is very extensive, arching on and on, spinning itself out in sensuous
convolutions.

Typical of the Baroque composer's conception of emotion in music
was his use of the doctrine of the affects. He often aimed to invest each
movement, aria, or chorus with one basic feeling or mood, and deliber-
ately structured his materials to produce homogeneity and oneness of
mood. Individual items display uniform meter and tempo; a single melodic
idea, activated by a simple rhythmic pattern, sufficed as the basis for a
composition. The result was a compact form of singular emotional thrust.

As implied above, the prevailing texture of Baroque music was polyphonic as it had been in the Renaissance. But there was one vital difference:
whereas the tonal underpinning for Renaissance polyphony was essentially

modal, that of the mature Baroque was based on a fully developed major-minor key system. And though polyphony predominated, homophony was gaining in importance. Beginning with the monody of early Italian Baroque opera with its rhetorical melody supported by block chords, and ending with the dissonant chordal combinations of J. S. Bach, homophony grew in influence. Jean-Philippe Rameau said that "Melody is born of harmony." With his book The Treatise of Harmony, he ultimately codified the major-minor harmonic system and firmly established the function of the chord within this system. His discussion of the principles of figured bass showed how far the development of harmony based on the major-minor system had come. All of this had profound influence for the next century and a half, for that system was at the core of most Rococo, Classical, and Romantic music. In fact, it can be said that Rameau's Treatise of Harmony (1722), Johann Joseph Fux's book on counterpoint titled Gradus ad Parnassum (1725), and J. S. Bach's Well Tempered Clavier were fundamental to music education for well over a century.

Among the larger "aggregate" vocal works, opera, oratorio, cantata, and the Mass predominated. Within these, the aria da capo, the choral fugue, and the accompanied chorale were standard fixtures. The chorale itself occupied a central position in the Baroque period. It was identified with the Reformation — one of the most revered chorale tunes is Martin Luther's "A Mighty Fortress is Our God" — and was at the heart of German Protestant music. The chorale as treated by J. S. Bach shows an ideal balance between linear and vertical forces. Each of its four melodic parts displays innate independence and beauty, while the chords resulting from the confluence of these parts are rock-solid. The Bach chorales are the perfect embodiment of the Baroque major-minor system and to this day serve as models for the study of the harmony of that period.

Instrumental music was well represented by several aggregate forms: the solo concerto, the concerto grosso, the sonata, the overture, and the suite. Within single movements, the fugue (often prefaced by a prelude), theme and variations, chaconne and passacaglia, binary dance forms, toccata, and the fantasia were favored. J. S. Bach regarded the fugue as a constant challenge throughout his creative life. The Well Tempered Clavier, Book 1 and Book 2, each consisting of 24 preludes and fugues written in all the major and minor keys, is a compendium of the expressive possibilities inherent in these structures.

The most widely used instruments were those of the string family, the harpsichord, the clavichord, the flute, the recorder, and the great church organ. Performance standards were high as represented by great composer-players such as Corelli, Telemann, Froberger, Rameau, Marchand, and J. S. Bach. Coloristic writing, begun in the Renaissance, advanced steadily while instrumental timbre as an element in composition gained in importance. The brilliant writing for the clarin trumpet by J. S. Bach was typical. The use of instruments for musical imagery — hunting horns, posthorns, birdcalls, storms — flourished.

Improvisation reached an extraordinary peak of refinement. Not only were singers, violinists, and others expected to ornament their given melodic parts extensively, but keyboard players realized full chordal and contrapuntal textures from a figured bass line. J. S. Bach, on his visit to Potsdam, is known to have improvised a three-part ricercare on a theme provided by Frederick the Great, himself no mean player of the flute.

The Baroque style, beginning as a reaction to the Renaissance, ultimately assimilated and transformed to its own purpose much of the materials and ways of thinking introduced in the previous century. The secular spirit of Renaissance humanism led to the flowering of a vital and colorful instrumental style, while the sincerity of the Reformation and the brilliance of the Counter-Reformation resulted in the drama and poignancy of Baroque church music. Super-sophisticated polyphonic structures of the Renaissance became, in the Baroque, incisive imitative structures informed by superb technical craft while at the same time expressing vivid emotional states. Thus, in its search for its own directions, the Baroque rejected what it could not use but accepted what it needed from the Renaissance. All the while, within its unique nature were present tendencies which would be grasped and re-formed in later styles.

THE MUSICK FOR THE ROYAL FIREWORKS

George Frederick Handel (1685-1759)

The Royal Fireworks Music is not an example of Baroque program music; it is ceremonial music of the most regal sort. Its composition was occasioned by the ceremonies in London (1749) celebrating the peace of Aix-la-Chapelle that ended the War of the Austrian Succession. The reports of the huge crowd of 12,000 attending the rehearsal and causing a mammoth traffic jam on London bridge, and the incident of the fire in the pavilion at the performance and display, are well known. But the quality of the brilliant music and especially the numbers and disposition of the players interest the music lover. There were 100 musicians at Green Park at the occasion, of which 43 were strings and 57 winds, including 24 oboes, 12 bassoons, 9 trumpets, and 9 horns! To the sophisticated modern ear tempered by the ideally balanced orchestras of Mozart, Haydn, Mendelssohn, and Debussy this preponderance of winds perhaps seems gauche. But there can be little doubt that the music could be easily heard by the massed outdoor audience.

Original orchestra: 3 first horns, 3 second horns, 3 third horns; 3 first trumpets, 3 second trumpets, 3 third trumpets; 3 pairs of kettledrums; 12 first oboes, 8 second oboes, 4 third oboes; 8 first bassoons, 4 second bassoons; and strings.

Structure: All dances — beginning with the Bourrée — are in binary form: A:‖:B:‖

OUVERTURE

LA PAIX

LA RÉJOUISSANCE

MENUET

MENUET

FOR DISCUSSION

1. Considering the circumstances of its composition and performance in
    1749, to what extent are modern arrangements of the Fireworks
    Music — for the concert hall — justified? Listen to the modern revised
    version by Sir Hamilton Harty.

2. Within the Allegro movement many striking antiphonal effects are
    heard: usually strings and woodwinds in dialogue with brass and drums,
    but sometimes trumpets against horns. Was there a reason for this in
    the circumstances of the first performance? How does this tie in with
    the antiphonal style heard in the earlier instrumental and choral
    Baroque music of Gabrieli in Italy? Compare with Giovanni Gabrieli's
    Sonata pian'e forte.

3. In terms of harmony, the music overall is diatonic and simple. What
    little chromaticism there is usually occurs when the brass and drums
    do not play. What does this suggest about the limitations of these in-
    struments relative to the prevalent harmonic style of the Royal Fire-
    works Music?

4. Listen carefully to the opening of the Overture. You will note that the
    interpretation does not conform exactly to the notation: certain shorter
    notes are further shortened, suggesting the French fashion of the day,
    in which durational values were manipulated in performance to achieve
    a more individual manner. What kind of effect does this rhythmic
    manipulation achieve?

5. Two of the French titles, "La Paix" (peace) and "La Réjouissance"
    (rejoicing), obviously relate directly to the celebration of the peace
    attained at Aix-la-Chapelle. Though this of itself does not place the
    music in the category of descriptive program music as such, it does
    illustrate the Baroque doctrine of musical affect, where one mood is
    delineated within one movement. Contrast the relation of title to effect
    in these two movements with the Battle Symphony by Beethoven and the
    1812 Overture by Tchaikovsky. Consider the social background for
    each of these three pieces and its effect on the music.

CONCERTO, OP. 8, NO. 4, "WINTER" (FROM "THE SEASONS")

Antonio Vivaldi (c. 1675-1741)

From 1703 to 1740 Vivaldi taught intermittently at the Conservatorio dell'
Ospedale della Pietà in Venice. There he wrote numerous concertos for
the students at the orphanage. The Concerto given in Score Sketch here is
typical of these pieces. It is lively and instructive, and the orchestral
parts do not require virtuosity.

Score Indications:

A sonnet entitled "Winter," sometimes attributed to Vivaldi, accompanies
this concerto. The Italian phrases appearing on the score and translated
below are taken from this sonnet. A translation of the entire sonnet follows.

m. 4.   Agghiacciato tremar tra nevi algenti: to shiver, frozen in the
snow and ice

m. 12.   Al severo spirar d'orrido vento: battered by a terrible wind's
harsh blow

m. 22.   Correr battendo i piedi ogni momento: to run, stamping your feet
every moment

m. 47.   E pel soverchio gel battere i denti: and from such cold your teeth
chatter

m. 64.   Passar dal foco i dì quieti e contenti mentre la pioggia fuor bagna
ben cento: to spend quiet and contented days by the fire while the
rain outside soaks things through and through

m. 82.   Caminar sopra il ghiaccio: to walk over the ice

m. 106. E a passo lento per timor di cader, girsene intenti: and with slow
step for fear of falling, walk intently

m. 121. Gir forte, sdrucciolar,...: to move on strongly, to slip and ...

m. 129. Cader a terra: fall to the ground

m. 132. Di nuovo ir sopra 'l ghiaccio e correr forte: to start again over
the ice and run hard

m. 170. Sin ch' il ghiaccio si rompe, e si disserra: until the ice breaks
and a path opens

m. 182. Sentir uscir dalle ferrate porte Scirocco, Borea: to feel issuing
from the iron gates the southeast wind (Sirocco), the north wind

m. 201. E tutti i venti in guerra: and all the winds at war

m. 228. Quest' è il verno, ma tal, che gioia apporte: This is winter, but
it also brings joys

"Winter" (translated by Dr. Martin Robbins)

Shivering, frozen in the snow and ice,
Battered by a terrible wind's harsh blow,
Stamping your feet, to run while time seems slow;
And from such cold your chattering teeth freeze;
To spend, content by the fire, quiet days
While the rain outside soaks things through and through;
To walk over ice with pace so slow,
Afraid to fall; to go, looking for ways
To move on strongly; to slip to the earth;
To start again on the ice; to run headlong
Until the ice breaks up and opens a path;
To feel, from the iron gates issuing,
The southeast, north, all the winds' warring breath:
This is winter, but joys it also brings.

(Note: The English version is also a sonnet.)

Solo: Violin

Orchestra: First and second violins, violas, violoncellos, contrabasses.
Harpsichord plays bass line (continuo) and, in addition, realizes chords
indicated by the figured bass.

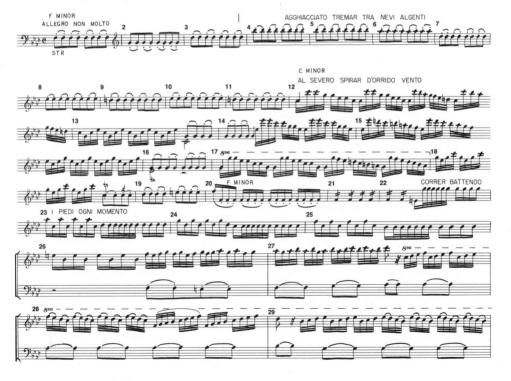

FOR DISCUSSION

1. To what extent does the solo concerto lend itself to descriptive music as exemplified in the "Winter" concerto? Does the homogeneity of string sound and the exclusion of all other orchestral timbres enhance or hinder the program idea in this work?

2. How are the virtuosic violin techniques used for imagery? The usual relationship of solo to orchestra in the concerto is that of dramatic juxtaposition. Though this spirit of conflict and confrontation is not so strong in the Baroque concerto as it is in later Classical and Romantic concertos, it still is an effective structural force. Does the programmatic content of the "Winter" concerto help to create a feeling of dramatic juxtaposition? To this point, how would this concerto stand on its own without descriptive titles?

3. How does Vivaldi's handling of textures in this work compare with that of J. S. Bach in the C minor/D minor Concerto in this book? Contrast the two composers' use of counterpoint, rhythmic pattern, and harmonic scheme.

ET INCARNATUS EST
(FROM THE CREDO SECTION OF THE B MINOR MASS)

J. S. Bach (1685-1750)

The B Minor Mass stands as one of the supreme liturgical masterpieces of all time. The three choruses, beginning with No. 15, Et incarnatus est, are central to the whole mass. The Et incarnatus est is followed by the Crucifixus cast as an intense, chromatic chaconne in E minor, veering at the last moment into the relative key (G major) for the words et sepultus est. No. 17 answers the pathos of the two preceding items with the optimism of the Et resurrexit, in the bright key of D major. Thus does the inner triptych of the Mass form a beautifully rounded whole, worthy of separate performance in a concert setting less imposing than that of the formal Mass.

Performance forces: Violins 1 and 2; continuo (viol or cello, contrabass, organ); soprano 1 and 2, alto, tenor, bass.

38

FOR DISCUSSION

1. The musical means used by Bach to realize the sense of mystery in the
    Et incarnatus est are superb. First there is the instrumental scoring:
    violins etching a single, poignant line over a gently throbbing continuo.
    The sobbing dissonance on the second and third beats of the violin line
    seems to anticipate the tragic events following the incarnation. At m.
    4 and in each succeeding measure the five voice parts enter one by one
    beginning with the alto. Each articulates a descending broken chord.
    The combination of the ascetic string scoring and overlapping, stag-
    gered entrances of the chorus could not better portray the implications
    of this moment in the liturgy.

2. Note the entrance of the bass at m. 8. It begins as do the first four
    voice parts, outlining a downward broken chord. At the crossing into
    m. 9, the expected minor 3rd is compressed to a diminished 3rd. This
    effect is startling. The resulting note, B sharp, itself resolves unex-
    pectedly to B natural on the word est. In m. 9 the harmony thus be-
    comes unsettled and the listener senses a new key goal.

3. A strong cadence in F sharp minor (m. 20) finds the strings presenting
    their original motive. Voices enter as before, staggered and outlining
    chords, but this time with the tenor leading. Measure 27 shows a more
    unsettled chord feeling as the home key is approached. A strong ca-
    dence in the tonic key of B minor sounds at m. 39, bringing the tonality
    full circle.

4. After the uniform, agonized line of the string parts from the beginning,
    the last five measures show a surprising change of texture: the basses
    lead with the original figure, but soon they are imitated by the second
    violins and then the first violins in an intense unwinding of the musical
    thread. The last tonic chord, with the raised 3rd, achieves serenity
    and rest. It also functions as the perfect harmonic lead into E minor,
    the key of the following Crucifixus.

PRELUDE AND FUGUE NO. 2 IN C MINOR
(FROM "THE WELL TEMPERED CLAVIER," BOOK 2)

J. S. Bach (1685-1750)

Written in 1744 toward the close of Bach's life, Book 2 of The Well Tempered Clavier was cast in the same format as was Book 1 twenty-two years before. Each book contains 24 preludes and fugues, each in one of the 12 major and 12 minor keys, following the order of the ascending chromatic scale. Thus the first paired prelude and fugue are in C major, the second in C minor; the third pair is in D flat major, the fourth in C sharp minor, and so on. Such a systematic presentation points to a didactic purpose on the composer's part. It was indeed Bach's intention that these preludes and fugues should serve as instructional material for students of the clavier as well as illustrate the practicality of the tempered system of tuning. As with the Esercizi of Domenico Scarlatti for cembalo written in the same period, the Etudes for piano by Chopin in the Romantic period, and the Mikrokosmos by Bartók in our time, the pedagogic utility of these Bach pieces is transcended by their inherent beauty.

The C minor fugue given here displays extensive thematic transformation of its melodic materials. In this respect it is typical of Book 2 of The Well Tempered Clavier, which shows broader and deeper contrapuntal exploration than does Book 1.

> "His volant touch,
> Instinct through all proportions, low and high,
> Fled and pursued transverse the resonant fugue."
>
> Milton, Paradise Lost, Book II

Structure: Prelude in binary form A:‖:B:‖ and fugue in four voices

Chords: Roman and arabic numerals. The roman numeral indicates the scale degree the chord is built upon. An arabic numeral indicates either an inverted chord or an extended chord.

FOR DISCUSSION

The Prelude

1. How does Bach's clearly utilitarian purpose in composing The Well
    Tempered Clavier   affect one's appreciation of the music's inherent
    esthetic qualities? Is it better to listen simply to the beauty of the
    music without examining its intricate structure? In listening to the
    fugue, is it better to listen innocently to the ever-changing contrapuntal
    texture propelled by a driving beat? Or is it more rewarding to make
    oneself aware of, and to follow carefully, the journey of the subject as
    it travels from one voice to another?

2. Bach was intimately acquainted with the harpsichord and the clavichord
    and had a passing knowledge of the pianoforte, then in its infancy as an
    instrument. Since he titled both books The Well Tempered Clavier, the
    word clavier suggesting any stringed keyboard instrument of the time,
    we can assume the legitimacy of the performance of any of the "Forty-
    Eight" on any of the above three instruments. Which of these would
    best suit the interpretation of the C minor Prelude and Fugue from
    Book 2? In a good dictionary of music investigate the crucial difference
    in the manner of eliciting tone from the strings of these three keyboard
    instruments. Become aware of the resulting difference of timbre by
    listening to recordings or, better, to the instruments themselves in
    concert. Would the clavichord's and pianoforte's ability to produce
    gradations of tone (nuance) contribute to the interpretation of these
    pieces? On which of the three would the player best be able to achieve
    clarity of line in the dense texture of the fugue?

3. What is the esthetic relationship of this prelude to its fugue? Is there
    present here the same kind of organic connection or identity of mood

that exists between the movements of a Beethoven Sonata or the successive songs of a lieder cycle by Schubert or Brahms?

4. There being no tempo indications in this music, how does the performer arrive at an effective rate of speed? How does choice of tempo re-
late to the denseness of texture in the fugue and the problem of project-
ing clearly all that needs to be heard simultaneously? Should the prelude be played at the same tempo as the fugue?

5. In the prelude itself a lean, two-part texture prevails throughout, suggesting Bach's Two-Part Inventions written many years before. Given
this meager sonority, how is interest sustained in the music itself?
Does the shifting of the basic melodic idea back and forth from right to
left hand provide sufficient interest? What other means has the composer utilized?

6. Twenty-eight measures are spanned by the prelude. Of these only 10
are unquestionably in the tonic key, C minor. At other times the music
modulates to contrasted but related keys. How can the piece be said to
be in the key of C minor when much of the time it is in other keys?
What is the organizing principle behind Baroque tonality as exemplified
here?

7. Note the repeat marks at m. 12 and at m. 28 of the prelude. The prelude is clearly cast as a typical Baroque structure: two-part binary
dance form. In many of the other preludes in the "Forty-Eight" a kind
of improvised, free structure prevails. Typical is the C major prelude from Book 1. Which of the two types provides the better introduction to the fugal severities that follow? Investigate other preludes of
the "Forty-Eight" for their basic pattern. Also investigate this form
as used by Chopin in his twenty-four Preludes, Op. 28, and by Debussy
in his twenty-four Préludes. Listen to the preludes to the operas of
Wagner, Bizet, Verdi, and Puccini. How do preludes of this type
differ from those mentioned above?

The Fugue

1. Note the brevity and the plastic nature of the subject. It spans only one
measure and, outlining the tonic chord, it registers easily with the ear.
The transfer of the subject in the second measure of the fugue (m. 30)
shows a slight adjustment in shape: the first interval, originally a 3rd,
now becomes a 2nd.

2. Measure 36 finds the subject in the soprano slightly disguised rhythmi-
cally, though the tones are precisely those of the original form.

3. At mm. 42 and 43 the contrapuntal plot thickens as the subject appears
in three distinctly different shapes. While the soprano carries the subject in its original form, the tenor shows it with its note values doubled
(augmentation), while the bass enters with the subject upside down

(melodic inversion). All the while these entrances of the subject over-lap so that one begins before the other has finished (stretto). This shortening of the time span between successive entrances actually con-tinues in the next three measures, though the subject appears in its original note values and right-side-up.

4. Up to this point, through m. 46, the contrapuntal texture has been formed by no more than three voices sounding at one time. In m. 47, which finds the subject in the bass in augmentation, the fugue is in four voices; it remains in four voices to the end. The effect is one of dra-matic intensification. At m. 51 another tightening of entrances occurs (stretto), this time displaying great density because of the four voices that are now involved. The last two measures discontinue the thick polyphonic web. Instead, a dissonant broken chord (diminished seventh) leads to an emphatic homophonic cadence perfectly suited to unwind the accumulated energy.

CONCERTO FOR VIOLIN, OBOE, AND STRINGS (D MINOR)

CONCERTO FOR TWO KEYBOARD INSTRUMENTS AND STRINGS (C MINOR)

J. S. Bach (1685-1750)

Though the solo forces differ in these two concertos, and though each is set in a different minor key, the music is essentially the same for both. The setting of identical or near-identical music for different performance media was a common procedure in the Baroque period. With Bach's rigorous schedule of productive activity it was perhaps inevitable that he should often have transcribed his and other composers' works. This concerto and the Schubler Chorale No. 1, Wachet auf, ruft uns die Stimme (after the tenor chorus from Cantata No. 140), are typical examples of Bach's recasting of his own work. The Concerto for Four Keyboard Instruments in A minor, transcribed from a Concerto for Four Violins by Vivaldi, shows Bach's deep interest in the music of his contemporaries. But beyond the obvious utilitarian value that these transcriptions offered Bach, we can be certain that he derived great pleasure from conceiving and then hearing the same music in contrasted timbres. The following juxtaposition (on the same page) of both versions of the first movement from the double concerto will give you an opportunity to compare timbres. You will also see the necessary adjustments made by Bach in writing the same music first for paired single-staff instruments, and then for paired double-staff instruments.

Orchestra: Violins 1 and 2, violas, continuo (violoncello and contrabass).

50

FOR DISCUSSION: COMPARISONS

1. One obvious comparison to be made is that between the sustaining in-
    struments of the D minor version and the plucked, non-sustaining in-
    struments of the C minor version. Which version appears to carry out
    the compositional ideas better? Are there compensatory features in the
    non-sustaining, harpsichord version? Does the music as a whole sug-
    gest the need for dynamics such as crescendo and diminuendo? If so,
    which version can better realize this type of dynamic scheme? Or do
    the typical terraced dynamics of the Baroque period seem to apply?

2. Another comparison can be made between the two concertos in relation
    to the contrapuntal play between each pair of soloists. It is evident
    that the play of melodic parts is more clearly heard in the D minor
    version because of the strong contrast in timbre between the violin and
    the oboe. Does the fact that two harpsichords in the C minor version
    display identical timbre hinder this play of contrapuntal parts? In the
    two-harpsichord version are there features which compensate for the
    lack of contrasting timbre?

3. A particularly noteworthy characteristic trait of the Baroque concerto
    grosso is the disposition of a small number of instruments (concertino)
    against a massed orchestra (ripieno). Typical of this arrangement are
    the concerti grossi of J. S. Bach, Corelli, and Vivaldi. Though not
    classified as examples of the concerto grosso, the concertos given here
    do feature the juxtaposition of small with large forces. Which of the
    two versions better illustrates this juxtaposition? Which provides the
    superior contrast of timbre: solo violin with solo oboe against massed
    strings, or paired harpsichords against massed strings? Compare
    both versions with the six Brandenburg Concertos by J. S. Bach.
    Which version comes closest to the timbral juxtaposition heard in the
    Brandenburg Concerto No. 5? In the Brandenburg Concerto No. 6?

4. In comparing the two versions of the above concerto you will see that
    the transposed right-hand parts for the two keyboardists are exactly
    those played by the violin and oboe soloists. Assuming that the violin-
    and-oboe version came first and that its single solo lines matched to
    the material of the massed strings form a highly satisfactory whole,
    what of the left-hand parts for harpsichord? Do they consist only of
    supportive "fill"? Does the composer resort to the obvious solution of
    having these left-hand parts simply double the lower string parts of the
    orchestra? Compare the solo parts in both concertos at mm. 9-12,
    20-22, and 27-32.

PART III CLASSICISM

The term "classical" is misused when it is applied to the whole field of art music; it is an admirable term for the music of the last half of the eighteenth century. For the ideal of composers at that time was music possessed of balance, symmetry, logic of statement, clarity, and elegance: precisely those virtues so often seen in the classic art and literature of ancient Greece and Rome. The universal simplicity of the Parthenon, of the writings of Socrates and Euclid, was recalled in the poised simplicity of musical classicism.

It was in the sphere of musical form that these virtues could best be realized. In fact, it was in the late Classical period that "absolute" music as represented by the symphony, concerto, sonata, and string quartet evolved to the point where it became the paragon for many later composers.

The basic structures of Haydn, Mozart, Boccherini, Clementi, and the young Beethoven show superb unity. The balance between unity and variety and of the parts to the whole is ideal. The favored structural patterns were those within the aggregate instrumental sonata: first-movement development form, rondo, theme and variations, minuet with trio, and the smaller ternary forms. Though vocal forms such as opera and the Mass were very important, it was in the "absolute" structures that composers could best achieve classic ideals.

Attesting to the importance of instrumental forms in the Classical period is the fact that Haydn wrote well over 100 symphonies and 83 string quartets. Mozart, in the short span of his life, produced 41 symphonies, upwards of 20 string quartets, and over 50 pieces in the solo concerto style.

The quality of certain instruments underwent significant improvement toward the close of the period. The pianoforte, for example, after nearly a century of development, challenged the harpsichord for supremacy. The development of the iron frame was only a few years away (Boston, 1825). This and the gradual expansion of its range through the addition of keys would make it the unchallenged favorite solo instrument in the Romantic age.

Clarinets, oboes, bassoons, and trumpets were refined technically. Thus the effective and unique scoring for instruments attained in the Baroque could now be enlarged in scope. With instruments more flexible than before, composers could now buttress their symphonic argument with more interesting wind parts. The literature for solo instruments also expanded in scope and in variety as can be seen in the many sonatas for pianoforte written by Haydn, Mozart, Clementi, and Beethoven.

Perhaps of paramount importance, the concert orchestra evolved into what is still the foundation of the orchestra today. The late Classical orchestral scoring for flutes, oboes, clarinets, bassoons, trumpets, horns, timpani in pairs, balanced by a fully developed string choir of violins, violas, cellos, and contrabasses, is the core of the Romantic, Impressionistic, and twentieth-century orchestra.

Of the several elements constituting Classical music, none was more important than texture. There was a decided and crucial shift away from the earlier elaborate polyphonic textures to simpler, more immediate homophonic textures. Rather than the predominantly dense, horizontal textures of the Baroque featuring intricate weaving of multiple melodic lines, the Classical period preferred vertical textures, with melody supported by chords. A single melody was now given predominance over other supportive elements, usually consisting of block or arpeggiated chords. The result was a new directness of impact, a clarity of melodic definition, and, most important, strong key relationships providing a cohesive undercurrent for the formal patterns being articulated.

All of this accorded perfectly with the attitude of Mozart and Haydn toward polyphony. Both were expert contrapuntists, but they were dubious about the continued value of polyphony. In this attitude they were joined by the English historian Burney and by the French philosopher-composer Jean Jacques Rousseau. It was the French philosopher who said of polyphonic devices that they "reflect disgrace on those who had the patience to construct them."

Melody in the Classical period was less complicated than in the Baroque. Baroque melody not only tended to be dotted with ornaments, but often was jagged in contour, using wide intervallic leaps. Classical melody sported fewer ornaments and was simple in outline, time and time again tracing elemental triadic shapes. Its phrases often fit neatly into a four-measure frame, punctuated by strong harmonic cadences. As a result, Classical melodies are easy to recognize even in transformation, as in the variation and development forms of the period.

In a like way Classical rhythms were more regular and fluid than Baroque. Syncopation was much less prominent and the downbeat was much emphasized. Because chord changes tended to coincide with the expected strong beats of the measure, the whole rhythmic effect tended to be regular and stable.

As to the emotional impact of Classical music, there can be little doubt that what is often felt by the listener is a kind of objective idealism, a deep satisfaction drawn from the very perfection of the ideally balanced structures. Mood and atmosphere usually are secondary, bowing always to the power of persuasive musical argument. Structure is what counts, not atmosphere. In short, Classical music appeals to the Apollonian side of our natures, striking a responsive chord in that unshadowed realm of our personality, that part of us which cherishes the serene though naive certainty of the essential beauty and positive quality of life.

Once having recognized this basic truth, one must be aware that it is not the whole reality. Dionysius had his word too, especially in the late Classical style of Haydn and Mozart — and in the works of Beethoven. The idea of "Sturm und Drang" (storm and stress), originating with the dramatist Friedrich Klinger (1752-1831), invaded the musical realm. Haydn's "Trauer" Symphony, No. 44, and his C Minor Symphony, No. 95, display intense passion. The first movements of the pianoforte concertos Nos. 20 and 24 by Mozart, both in minor keys, are highly subjective, expressing perhaps the inner travail of his later years. The patetico instrumental style was in vogue, as can be seen by the title Beethoven gave to his C minor pianoforte sonata, Op. 13: "Pathétique."

This personal kind of musical expression obviously carried enormous implications for later composers of the Romantic century. Not so obvious is that it was at least partly derived from the Baroque, particularly as that earlier style related to the doctrine of the affects. Baroque intensity of personal expression had its counterpart within the Classical style. Thus selected emotional factors from the Baroque were assimilated by the classicists. In their turn these factors would crop up in later styles.

SYMPHONY NO. 104, "LONDON" (1795), FINALE

Franz Joseph Haydn (1732–1809)

The twelve Salomon Symphonies, of which this is the last, occupy a position of summary and ultimate perfection in the genre as attained by Haydn. In that sense they are equivalent to other terminal masterworks such as the Symphonies Nos. 39, 40, and 41 by Mozart, the Ninth by Beethoven, Schubert's Winterreise cycle of lieder, and Verdi's last two operas, Otello and Falstaff. In its matchless fusing of structure with idea, Haydn's "London" Symphony achieves ideal balance within an exemplary classical style.

Bartók quotes the Croatian peasant song that underlies Haydn's first theme in the Finale:

Structure: Sonata allegro form with coda

72

DOMINANT PREPARATION

80

THEME I-A

84

CODA THEME I-C

FOR DISCUSSION

1. Haydn was fond of making one melodic idea (motive) do for several
    themes in his sonata allegro forms. For example, the core idea
    heard in the first violins in mm. 3-6 underlies that part of the transi-
    tion beginning at m. 31. A glance at the second measure of the develop-
    ment section (m. 119) shows the same motive playing an important role
    there also. Does this point to Haydn the conservative, looking back at
    the unithematic structures of the Baroque? Baroque composers often
    derived extensive structures from one trenchant melodic idea. Or was
    Haydn here simply looking for greater unity and motivic cohesion?

2. The orchestra in this symphony typifies the essential instrumental
    core that has been the basis of the orchestra to our day: woodwinds,
    brass, and drums in pairs, balanced by a full string choir. How does
    Haydn handle these instrumental elements? Does any one group pre-
    dominate? Considering that the horns, trumpets, and timpani play to-
    gether much of the time, what kind of role do they play: melodic,
    rhythmic, dynamic, harmonic?

3. Though the formal pattern followed is sonata allegro, much associated
    with dramatic music, this finale suggests a gay, blithe atmosphere.
    Dramatic moments providing contrast do exist, however. One of these
    begins at m. 167, at the passage leading to the entrance of Theme 1 in
    the recapitulation. How does Haydn achieve the sudden darkening of
    mood in these measures? Where does the motivic material come from?
    What is the harmonic "feel" of the passage? Is there anything unusual
    in the harmonic transition (mm. 191-194) to the first tonic chord of the
    recapitulation? Why the dynamic marking of *pp* at m. 191?

4. Haydn seldom if ever brings back themes exactly as before. Compare
    and discuss Themes 1 and 3 as they appear in both exposition and re-
    capitulation.
    Theme 1: exposition, m. 3; recapitulation, m. 195.
    Theme 2: exposition, m. 84; recapitulation, m. 247.

CLARINET QUINTET, K. 581, FOURTH MOVEMENT

Wolfgang Amadeus Mozart (1756-1791)

". . . Count Hadik has invited me to perform for him Stadler's quintet . . ."
This Quintet was written in 1789 in Vienna for Mozart's friend, the clari-
netist Anton Stadler. Both the Quintet and the later Clarinet Concerto, K.
622, also written for Stadler, require consummate musicianship. This
attests to Mozart's respect for Stadler the artist. The humorous nickname
Mozart gave him, "Redcurrant Face," points to a warm, human relationship. There is little doubt that it was Stadler who fully revealed to Mozart
the tone and technical potential of the clarinet.

Performance medium: Clarinet in A, violin 1, violin 2, viola, violoncello

Structure: Theme and variations

Chords: Roman and arabic numerals. The roman numeral indicates the
scale degree the chord is built upon. An arabic numeral indicates either
an inverted chord or an extended chord. L (leading tone) indicates the
seventh degree of the scale when it is a minor 2nd below the tonic.

ANALYTICAL NOTES

Theme, m. 1: Note the plastic simplicity of this tune; it will be easy to recall in the course of the variations. First and second violins start with the tune in 3rds. The clarinet enters at mm. 3 and 7 for harmonic cadences only.

m. 9: Dialogue between first violin and viola provides legato contrast to the preceding staccato idea.

m. 13: Initial idea returns in the first violin, this time with the high-ranging viola shadowing it in 3rds. The second violin enters two beats later, imitating the first violin. The structure of the theme itself is two-part binary form (A-B). The first eight measures (part A) are balanced by the following eight measures (part B). However, the brief return of the first motive at m. 13 also suggests a circular ternary structure.

Variation 1, m. 17: The clarinet provides elaborate melodic gymnastics as a background to the strings, which are carrying the tune. At m. 25 all reference to the theme except for its harmonic foundation disappears for four measures. The clarinet continues to elaborate its leaping line. Slipping in under the clarinet part, the tune returns in the strings to round out Variation 1.

Variation 2, m. 33: The original contour of the theme disappears completely while the harmony remains. A new melodic shape is heard in the first violins. Below, the second violin and the viola provide kinetic propulsion through the use of a repeated triplet figure. Note the surprising accents on weak beats throughout the first violin part. In contrast to its active role in Variation 1, the clarinet here provides only a few perfunctory figures. Most of the action lies in the string parts.

Variation 3, m. 49: This variation finds the musical thought even further removed from the original theme than it was in Variation 2. The harmony darkens as A major becomes A minor. Though the mode changes from major to minor, original chord relationships remain intact and the theme's binary structure is retained. Thus two vital elements of the theme's structure remain intact. The viola leads, playing an undulating line prophetic of the early nineteenth-century lyric style. Again the clarinet plays a secondary but not unimportant role. In the hollow voice of its chalumeau register it articulates simple broken chords, providing a velvety cushion for the viola's line. The first violin momentarily assumes the lead at m. 57.

Variation 4, m. 65: After having gone underground in Variations 2 and 3, the original tune returns in Variation 4. It reappears in its original shape in the first violin. The clarinet, which has taken a subsidiary role for the previous two variations, now bursts in with virtuosic sixteenth-note figuration backing up the tune. As if sparked by the dazzling activity of the clarinet, the first violin at m. 69 goes forth on its own with scintillating figuration. In the last four measures Variation 4 ends as it began with the tune in the first violin while the clarinet spins out its lively line.

Bridge, m. 81: The four brief measures of this bridge passage are very important. Because the following variation will be presented in a tempo and mood markedly different from what went before, special preparation is needed. Harmonically this passage consists of little more than a strong cadence formula ending with an expectant dominant seventh chord under a fermata. This holds back the propulsion of Variation 4 enough so that the ear can easily adjust to the adagio tempo to follow.

Variation 5, m. 85: In this leisurely, expressive adagio can be heard the essential cantabile style of the Classical period. No reference is made to the original tune but its harmonic underpinning again is retained. This chordal structure now generates entirely new melodic material shared by the first violin and the clarinet in dialogue. Note the rising flourishes in the clarinet at mm. 93 and 95.

Bridge, m. 101: Just as the bridge passage in m. 81 led naturally to the quiet Variation 5, so does this five-measure bridge prepare the way for what is to come. Two soft and hesitant figures lead to an expansive phrase ending on a suspenseful half cadence.

Variation 6, m. 106: Variation 6 not only shows the theme in a new guise but serves as a brilliant finale as well. There is a gearing up of tempo from the original theme: allegretto now becomes allegro. In addition to this increase of speed, the overall formal structure is considerably expanded from that of the original theme and the previous five variations. It now spans 36 measures. Several unique touches deserve special notice. Beginning at m. 109 the cello, which up to this point was given melodic materials of minimal interest, now plays an important, bustling bass line. Later (mm. 129–137) it plays a vital held note anchoring the music firmly in the home key, A major. Twice Mozart injects fluid, chromatic chords into the otherwise bland diatonic harmonic scheme (mm. 118–121 and 126–129). The variation ends with a fragment from the initial tune tossed back and forth in the strings.

SEVENTH SYMPHONY, OP. 92, FIRST MOVEMENT

Ludwig van Beethoven (1770–1827)

This symphony, the "dance" symphony, was finished by Beethoven in 1812, but was not performed until the following year in Vienna. The introduction is extremely long, covering 62 measures. After this Beethoven establishes the characteristic rhythmic pattern of the first movement, ♩.♫ ♩.♫ , and its robust energy remains unflagging until the end of the movement.

Structure: Sonata allegro, with introduction and extended coda

Orchestra:

2 Flutes (FL)   Violins (VL 1, 2)

2 Oboes (OB)   Viola (VA)

2 Clarinets (CL)   Violoncello (VC)

2 Bassoons (BN)   Contrabass (CB)

2 Horns (HN)

2 Trumpets (TR)

2 Timpani (TIMP)

FOR DISCUSSION

1. Note the rich modulation scheme in the introduction: from A major
    through C major and F major to the final goal, A major. The swing
    from the tonic, A major, to these keys is striking. But despite the
    character of these relationships, the emphasis on the tonic root is very
    strong; the explorations revolve around the tonic at the distance of a
    3rd.

2. At the beginning of the exposition section, one basic rhythmic figure is
    established, and will predominate throughout the remainder of the
    movement. How does Beethoven's systematic use of this rhythmic
    idea compare with the many Baroque pieces organized along mono-
    rhythmic lines? Compare this symphony with the Brandenburg Concer-
    tos Nos. 1 and 2 by J. S. Bach. Given this unremitting rhythmic con-
    sistency, how do both composers achieve the necessary variety with
    other structural elements?

3. In m. 164 note that Theme 3 is derived from Theme 1. This is a new
    theme in spite of its derivation. The classic sense of contrast between
    tonic and dominant is maintained here by Beethoven. The important
    point is that the second theme and the closing theme of this movement
    remain in the dominant, allowing for the important psychological "fall"
    back to the tonic when the exposition is repeated.

4. Note the use of canonic entrances (based on Theme 1) at the beginning
    of the development, which a more formal fugal style would demand.
    Consider possible reasons why the composer chose to open the devel-
    opment section in this manner.

5. Note the key of the restatement of Theme 1 in the recapitulation (m.
    301). Is this key area the expected one at this juncture of the form?
    How does this key strengthen the dynamism of the overall harmonic
    motion?

6. In m. 401 note the new uses of thematic material introduced into what
    proves to be a rather extensive coda. In the low strings there begins
    a two-bar chromatic ostinato derived from Theme 1, which covers 22
    measures before cadencing. What is the dramatic and musical effect
    of this ostinato?

PART IV ROMANTICISM

If the Classical period was primarily characterized by restraint and balance, the Romantic period (1800-1900) was marked by emotional extremes and the uninhibited expression of the self.

Romanticism meant exploration and expansion both within and without. As the Romantic tone poet delved within himself to discover unsuspected areas of sensibility, his musical style expanded to express previously submerged feelings. Schumann, in an essay written in 1831, explored the trichotomy of his inner personality and, anticipating modern psychology, gave each segment of his psychic life its own incarnation: Eusebius the gentle dreamer, Florestan the Dionysian seer, and Master Raro, the intermediary between the two. Eusebius and Florestan later appeared as tone portraits in the Carnaval, Op. 9, for piano solo. Berlioz, prodded by his passion for the Shakespearean actress Harriet Smithson, vented his own exotic fantasies in the Symphonie Fantastique.

The outside world too was thoroughly explored by the Romantic composer. He gave expression to the actual physical world surrounding him and to the related arts such as literature and painting.

Nationalistic music flowered. Composers such as Glinka, Smetana, and Sibelius captured with tone and rhythm the very heartbeat of their native land. The Russian Glinka with his opera A Life for the Tsar, and the Czech Smetana with his opera The Bartered Bride, inflamed their compatriots with pride for the homeland. Others, such as Mendelssohn, Tchaikovsky, and Dvořák brought back musical souvenirs from lands not their own. The Scotch and Italian Symphonies by Mendelssohn were written after extensive visits to Scotland and Italy. Dvorak, after his years in America, brought back the familiar Symphony From the New World, and the not so familiar but exquisite String Quartet in F major, called the "American."

Like Beethoven, the Romantic composer thought of himself as a Tondichter (tone poet). He was challenged not only by the poetry of tone but by the poetry of words. In fact, several Romantic composers were superior writers. Schumann, Berlioz, and Weber were immensely effective as music critics and essayists. Wagner wrote the libretti for all of his own operas and also penned innumerable essays and pamphlets on a wide variety of topics. Berlioz and Rimsky-Korsakov produced books on instrumentation that are important to students of the orchestra even today.

But even more important than their own work in letters was the Romantic composers' acquaintance with and use of the work of poets, novelists, and dramatists. The immense wealth of lieder set to poems by Goethe, Schiller, Heine, Eichendorff, and others attests to the Romantic composer's attraction to great literature. The lieder cycles by Schubert, Schumann, Brahms, and Wolf show an ideal coalescence of text with tone.

Great literary themes from drama, from the novel, and from fable found their way into opera, lied, and instrumental program music. Goethe's Faust alone was the inspiration for many works, including

Gounod's opera Faust, Berlioz' dramatic legend The Damnation of Faust, the Faust Symphony by Liszt, and the Faust Overture by Wagner. Cervantes' picaresque novel Don Quixote inspired a symphonic poem by Richard Strauss, and many of Shakespeare's plays were transformed into musical works. German mythological themes found their way into Wagnerian opera, while the monumental Finnish epic Kalevala suffused much of the music of Sibelius.

Thus the Romantics explored constantly, both within and around themselves, expanding their mode of expression until it seemed that very little could not be represented in tone: from the conjugal love murmurings of Wagner in his Siegfried Idyll, to the hothouse passion of Berlioz' Symphonie Fantastique; from the "Ballet of the Hatching Chicks" in Mussorgsky's Pictures at an Exhibition, to the Totentanz (Dance of Death) by Liszt; from the "Orgy of the Brigands" in Berlioz' symphony titled Harold in Italy, to Desdemona's "Ave Maria" in Verdi's opera Otello.

To accommodate their new mode of expression, composers enlarged upon and transformed the musical materials at hand. Harmony became freer, with dissonance often specifically used for novel effect. In the works of the later Romantics of the Wagnerian school, dissonant chords tended not to resolve immediately to a proper consonance. Instead would come another dissonant harmony leading the musical thought on and on. Chords of the 9th, 11th, and 13th were consciously dispersed through luxuriant textures to gain maximum sensual effect. Range and dynamics became ever more powerful agents for achieving high passion and color: there were more highs and lows, more louds and softs.

Rhythm became looser, with rubato tempo much in evidence. Along with rhythm, melody became less segmented than it had been in the Classical period; it became expansive and lovely for its own sake.

Except for the tone poem, the lied, and the character piece for piano, the forms were essentially those of the Classical period, but they were constantly refashioned through the use of new structural elements. However, the scope of Romantic forms changed radically. Whereas a symphony by Haydn would perhaps span fifteen or twenty minutes, those by the later Romantics such as Bruckner and Mahler sometimes lasted an hour or more. On the other hand, the character pieces by Chopin and Schumann often could be measured in seconds.

Instruments, and the orchestra itself, were modified enormously in order to accommodate the advances in expression. Wagner invented a family of tubas, the so-called Wagnertuben, and through them invested the voice of the dragon Fafner in his opera Siegfried with a new dimension of horror. The piano, once it acquired its iron frame at the hands of Babcock of Boston in 1825, began to match the orchestra itself in power and brilliance.

In the area of performance, virtuosos such as Liszt, Paganini, Jenny Lind, and Johann Strauss, Jr. caught the imagination of continents by symbolizing the creative power of the human spirit. The social lot of both composers and performers improved considerably; they were now their own men, free agents who were limited only by their talent and its acceptance by the public.

In sum, then, Romantic music represented exploration, variety, and the expansion of expressive horizons. Subjectivity routed the rational detachment of the past and the composer's immediate emotional condition predominated.

BALLADE IN G MINOR, OP. 23

Frederick Chopin (1810–1844)

"The G minor Ballade is the Odyssey of Chopin's soul; in it are the surge and thunder of the Poet." Thus did the critic James Huneker characterize this Ballade. There is no explicit program for any of the four Ballades written by Chopin. Chopin said, however, that the Lithuanian poems of the Polish poet Adam Mickiewicz had influenced the creation of the Ballades. We can be quite certain that the imagery and scenes from the poems were somehow translated into tone and rhythm.

Structure: Rondo

Konrad Wollenrad (beginning stanza of Section III), by Adam Mickiewicz (translated by Dr. Martin Robbins):

He kissed the holy book of laws,
Finished his prayer, took from the commander
Both the sword and the great Cross,
Full of might. Though a cloud of care
Weighed on him, he lifted his face
With pride. As he looked, his eyes flashed,
Joy and anger contending in his gaze,
While a rare smile, quite faint, then passed
Like a gleam that breaks the dawn asunder,
Portending both sunset and thunder.

FOR DISCUSSION

1. As stated on the introductory page there is no explicit program in-
    volved in this Ballade, though Chopin may well have had certain scenes
    or situations in mind during its composition. Does the music lend it-
    self to imagery? If so, in what way? Would it be best to experience
    this work as an example of absolute music? Since the Ballade is pref-
    aced by an introduction and punctuated by a sizable coda, might it pos-
    sibly have served as the first movement of a piano sonata? Compare
    it with the first movement of Chopin's Sonata in B Flat Minor, Op. 35.

2. In what ways — harmonic, melodic, rhythmic — is it possible to see
    Polish ethnic elements in the Ballade? Is there any hint of folk song
    or dance?

3. Examine the music for its inner divisions (see the analysis on the
    score). What is the balance between elements of unity and elements of
    variety? Does the composer bring themes back exactly as before?
    Compare Chopin's approach to the principles of unity and variety here
    with that found in the first movement of Beethoven's Seventh Symphony
    earlier in this book.

4. Chopin's reputation as "poet of the piano" was justified by his playing.
    His compositions employ superbly idiomatic writing for the piano.
    Compare the characteristic writing for piano in this Ballade with that
    in works by Beethoven, Schumann, Mendelssohn, and Schubert. To
    what extent is each composer affected by purely timbral considera-
    tions? Would it be possible to transcribe effectively the piano works
    of Chopin for orchestra? For string quartet?

CREDO IN UN DIO CRUDEL (FROM ACT 2 OF "OTELLO," 1886)

AVE MARIA (FROM ACT 4 OF "OTELLO," 1886)

Giuseppe Verdi (1813-1901)

The librettist for Otello was the opera composer and poet Arrigo Boito. The fact that Boito was a composer as well as a man of letters worked to Verdi's advantage. Verdi, who was extremely critical of librettists and had seldom been satisfied with the librettos of his earlier works, found in Boito a collaborator of the highest caliber. Otello, and Verdi's last opera Falstaff, also provided with a matchless libretto by Boito, are considered to be the composer's ultimate masterpieces.

Otello is based on the last three acts of Shakespeare's Othello, the Moor of Venice. Both the "Credo" and the "Ave Maria" are settings of words not found in the Shakespeare play. The original Boito text for these two arias integrates beautifully into the dramatic concept of the opera as a whole. The "Credo" is a kind of distillation of Iago's malevolent character as seen in Shakespeare's original:

Iago (to Roderigo):

Virtue! a fig! 'tis in ourselves that we are thus or thus. Our bodies are our gardens; to the which our wills are gardeners; so that if we will plant nettles, or sow lettuce, set hyssop and weed up thyme, supply it with one gender of herbs, or distract it with many, either to have it sterile with idleness or manured with industry, why, the power and corrigible authority of this lies in our wills.

Though there is no "Ave Maria" as such in the play, we know from Shakespeare that Desdemona has prayed:

Othello:
Have you pray'd to-night, Desdemona?

Desdemona:
Ay, my lord.

Othello:
If you bethink yourself of any crime
Unreconciled as yet to Heaven and grace,
Solicit for it straight.

Desdemona:
Alas, my lord, what do you mean by that?

Othello:
Well, do it, and be brief; I will walk by.
I would not kill thy unprepared spirit;
No; heaven forfend! I would not kill thy soul.

The contrast between the two major arias included here from the opera is marked. Iago represents ultimate human corruption; Desdemona is all innocence and love. Melody, harmony, orchestral color in each case work to deepen and intensify the characterization.

Translation of Iago's "Credo" (by Dr. Martin Robbins):

Iago (Watching Cassio leave):

Go now. Even now I see your plan.
Your demon drives you on,
and I am your demon.
And mine urges me on,
inexorable God I believe in.

I believe in a cruel God who created me
like himself, whom, in hate, I name.
I am born of a vile atom,
from the baseness of a germ.
I am a villain
because I am a man;
and feel the primal slime in me.
This is my faith! Truly!
I believe with a firm heart,
like the young widow at the altar,
that with the evil I think or that
begins with me I fulfill my fate.
I believe the just man is a comic mocker,
in the heart and in the face,
all that's in him lies:
A tear, a glance, a kiss,
honor and sacrifice.
And I believe iniquitous fate makes man a fool
from the germ and the cradle
to the worm and the grave.
Then death comes to mock us.
And then? And then — death, and nothingness.
Heaven is an old fable.

ANALYTICAL NOTES

1. The recitative portion of the "Credo" spans mm. 1-27. Note that
    severe, uncompromising octaves begin and end this section. Steady
    rhythm and a more lyric vocal line (mm. 30-57) mark a change to the
    aria style. The recitative style returns in mm. 58-70 and the mighty
    surge beginning at m. 71 punctuates the whole with a high note, full
    voice for the baritone and full sound for the orchestra.

2. Every structural element of the "Credo" is designed to illumine Iago's
    words. Each of the three motives is severe and vigorous, almost
    spartan in character. Together they perfectly portray the defiant arro-
    gance of Iago. The harmony is restlessly chromatic, constantly shift-
    ing from key to key. Note the startling change, up a minor 2nd, at
    the entrance of the second motive (m. 13). At the words "to feed the
    worm of death" (mm. 54-56) the stifled harmony is devastatingly sug-
    gestive, with the alternation of F sharp and G natural over the C sharp
    in the bass.

3. The orchestra is beautifully handled throughout. The brass writing is
    particularly effective. Note the tremendous rhythmic propulsion
    achieved through repeated brass chords at mm. 28, 36, 45, and 70.

Translation of Desdemona's "Ave Maria" (by Dr. Martin Robbins):

Hail Mary, full of grace,
Chosen among wives and virgins art thou,
Blessed be the fruit, O blessed woman,
Of thy womb, Jesus.
Pray for her, kneeling to adore Thee,
Pray for the sinner, and the innocent,
For the weak and subjugated, and for the powerful,
Also pitiable, show your pity.
Pray for one burdened and bowed by insult,
One with an ill-starred destiny.
For us, pray for us, pray
Always and at the hour of our death,
Pray for us, pray for us, pray . . .
Ave Maria . . .
nell' ora della morte.
Ave! . . . Amen!

Note: The "Ave Maria" as given here is the version any Italian at prayer
would use, not the original Latin. The entire translation is given, phrase
by phrase, at the end because it indicates Desdemona's agitated feelings of
foreboding, expressed by both words and music.

ANALYTICAL NOTES

1. Like the "Credo," the "Ave Maria" is cast in modified recitative-aria form. The recitative section spans mm. 1-11. Desdemona sings part of the words of the liturgical prayer on a single note, E flat. This is as consistent with early liturgical chant as it is with the early recitative style of the Baroque and Classical periods. Thus Verdi not only sets the right tone for the pious Desdemona but continues in the traditional operatic path as well.

2. The aria section proper spans mm. 12-38. Here the vocal line becomes thoroughly lyric while a steady but flexible beat is established. At m. 38 interesting things happen. The orchestra plays the same music as it did at the beginning of the recitative. But at the third measure (m. 40) it shifts over and plays what it did during the last part of the aria (mm. 29-35). All the while Desdemona sings two short phrases of the liturgy, and toward the close a luminous high A flat, dolcissimo. Thus the overall structure is as follows:

    Recitative: mm. 1-11
    Aria: mm. 12-38
    Combined elements of recitative and aria: mm. 38-55

3. There can be little doubt that Verdi wished to portray Desdemona as pure and innocent. Occurring as it does immediately before Otello's accusation and murder of Desdemona, the chaste "Ave Maria" serves to intensify the pathos. Accordingly, every structural element of the piece is designed to underline the simple and trusting character of the heroine. The orchestration is very simple: only the muted string choir plays. However, the bass is held in reserve for the entrance of Otello through the secret door after Desdemona has fallen asleep (see mm. 56-61). The use of strings alone contrasts strongly with the orchestra of the "Credo," which is highly diversified, emphasizing the powerful winds.

Both the "Credo" and the "Ave Maria" are cast in modified recitative-aria form. Though Verdi was aware of the operatic innovations of Wagner in the area of continuous melody and the leitmotif, he preferred to stick to the essentials of the traditional Italian number aria. Otello abounds in set pieces: the drinking song and the love duet of the first act are typical, as are the two arias given here. And while the orchestra in Otello is large and "symphonic," it never impinges on the supremacy of the vocal line.

SIEGFRIED IDYLL

Richard Wagner (1813-1883)

<u>Dedication to Cosima</u> (translated by Dr. Martin Robbins):

It was your high design, your sacrifice
That gave my work an ample place to grow,
Blessed by you to world-removed silence,
Where now my work's strength has steadily gained,
Transporting hero-world into an idyll,
From distant myths to the beloved homeland.
And now, a call of joy resounded through my songs:
"A son is born" — and Siegfried was his name.

For him and you I could give thanks in music,
Is there a lovelier prize for what you've done?
We always cherished within our home's confines
The quiet joy that now has turned into music.
Unmixed, this joy proved true to us,
Now may it smile friendly on our son,
Whatever we enjoyed in sounding bliss,
May, with your love, to him be open.

Through this poem Wagner showed his deep love and devotion for Cosima, the mother of his infant son Siegfried. The <u>Idyll</u> was performed on Cosima's birthday on the morning of December 25, 1870 on the staircase of their home in Triebschen bei Luzern. As the tone poem developed with its intertwined themes carrying up the staircase to her bedroom, Cosima's recognition of some of these themes must have affected her deeply. Indeed, the quality of the <u>Idyll</u> must have pleased Cosima as much as her husband's thoughtfulness. Wagner included several motives from his <u>Ring</u> opera <u>Siegfried</u> (1856-1869). That these motives were taken from the last scene in the third act, the passionate love scene of Siegfried and Brünnhilde, shows a delightful conjugal adroitness on the part of the composer. Surely this was not lost on Cosima.

<u>Structure</u>: Expanded ternary form: A-B-A'-Coda

A TEMPO, SEHR RUHIG
E MAJOR

BRUNNHILDE MOTIVE

128

B MAJOR (∇^9)

134

138

144

151

154

ANALYTICAL NOTES

1. The orchestra is one of near-chamber music proportions: except for the clarinets and horns, all the winds are single. (Part of the Idyll's content was taken from an early projected string quartet by Wagner.) However, despite the limited number of instruments, Wagner always manages to present his materials in fresh, luxuriant garb. Note how skillfully and unobtrusively Wagner introduces the winds beginning at m. 35.

2. Attesting to the chamber music quality of the score are the lovely solos for winds. See m. 91 for a long oboe solo in folk song style; m. 201 for another oboe solo carrying the principal theme; and the horn solo, with obbligati in various instruments, beginning at m. 259. The rather contrapuntal nature of the work allows each of the wind players opportunity to play individually rewarding music; this again suggests chamber music.

   The contrapuntal element in the Idyll reveals an extremely rich texture. Examine the first seven measures and note how the melodic parts for violas and cellos enhance the leading line in the first violins. At mm. 62-69 several motives come together to form a rich mosaic of contrapuntal figuration.

3. At m. 286 (A') begins a passage of great complexity. Three of the work's principal melodic ideas sound together in triple counterpoint. The violins carry the work's opening theme while the upper woodwinds play a version of the theme first heard at m. 150. Meanwhile, the oboe at m. 287 plays the Brünnhilde motive:

Despite this complexity, the effect is simple and direct, suffused with warm, romantic ardor.

4. The two principal themes of the Idyll (mm. 29–35 and mm. 148–168) are taken from Brünnhilde's music in the third act of the opera Siegfried as her love for Siegfried gradually awakens:

Brünnhilde's motive in the opera (given on page 155) does not assume a major role in the Idyll but intertwines itself around the principal themes at several points (see mm. 37-47 and 287 ff). The charming solo for the horn (mm. 259 ff.) with accompanying birdcalls in high woodwinds comes from the joyous last pages of the love scene in Siegfried.

SYMPHONIE FANTASTIQUE, OP. 14, FIFTH MOVEMENT

Hector Berlioz (1803-1869)

The Symphonie Fantastique is remarkable on many counts. Its date, 1830, is incredibly early when one considers the revolutionary, prophetic features of its structure and style. It was the first thoroughly cyclic work of the Romantic period, its basic theme (the idée fixe) occurring in each of five movements. The subject matter of the program is extraordinary for its time, encompassing everything from amorous yearnings and passion to a ghoulish decapitation at the guillotine followed by a brush with leering witches in a scene somewhere near hell. In this respect the Fantastique not only set the stage for Liszt's Totentanz, but also anticipated a great many late Romantic tone poems in the same genre: Mussorgsky's Night on Bald Mountain, Tchaikovsky's Francesca da Rimini, Wagner's Ride of the Valkyries (the prelude to Act 3 of the opera Die Walküre), and Saint-Saëns' Danse Macabre. In addition, details of rhythm, harmony, and structure in the music show an almost twentieth-century daring.

Berlioz wrote the work to depict the dreams of a sensitive young musician who, in a paroxysm of love-sick despair, has drugged himself with opium. The program for the work's fifth movement, titled "The Witches' Sabbath," is as follows:

> He dreams that he is present at a witches' dance, surrounded by horrible spirits, amidst sorcerers and monsters in many fearful forms, who have come to assist at his funeral. Strange sounds, groans, shrill laughter, distant yells which other cries seem to answer. The beloved melody is heard again but it has its noble and shy character no longer; it has become a vulgar, trivial, and grotesque kind of dance. She it is who comes to attend the witches' meeting. Friendly howls and shouts greet her arrival . . . She joins the infernal orgy . . . bells toll for the dead . . . a burlesque parody of the Dies irae . . . the witches' round dance . . . the dance and the Dies irae are heard at the same time.

Structure: Free fantasy

Orchestra:

Flute (FL)	4 Horns (HN)	Violins (VL 1, 2)
Piccolo (PIC)	2 Trumpets, 2 Cornets (TR)	Violas (VA)
2 Oboes (OB)	3 Trombones (TB)	Violoncellos (VC)
2 Clarinets (CL)	2 Tubas (TU)	Contrabasses (CB)
4 Bassoons (BN)		

4 Timpani (TIMP), Bass Drum (BD), 2 Bells

5. THE WITCHES' SABBATH

WITCHES' ROUND DANCE

FOR DISCUSSION

See discussion notes on page 170.

TOTENTANZ (FIRST VERSION, 1839-1840)

Franz Liszt (1811-1886)

Emil von Sauer, in the Peters edition of the Liszt Concertos, states that
". . . on beholding that picture (The Triumph of Death by Andrea Orcagna)
at Pisa in 1838, the 'Dies irae' theme of the ancient Chant . . . with a few
variations, at once came into his (Liszt's) mind." Perhaps we can safely
assume that Berlioz' essay in the bizarre, the fifth movement of the Symphonie Fantastique, also jumped into Liszt's mind at that moment; he had
arranged that work for piano solo in 1833.

     Whatever the artistic genesis of this work, it and the Symphonie
Fantastique represent basic attitudes and trends of the Romantic period as
a whole. For one, the Totentanz suggests imagery, though not so overtly
as does the Berlioz symphony. Second, in its diabolical technical demands
upon the pianist it is highly representative not only of Liszt's penchant for
virtuosic works but of brilliant music for instruments and voices by other
romantic composers. One thinks of Paganini's treatment of the solo violin,
Rossini's use of the voice, and Richard Strauss's compositions for the
virtuoso orchestra.

     In addition, this work, along with other pieces in this medium by
Liszt (the First and Second Piano Concertos, the Hungarian Fantasy) is
cast in one movement instead of the usual three. This illustrates the characteristic Lisztian compression of form. Finally, the use of the Dies irae
in the Totentanz is typical of the Romantic artist's fascination with the
veiled past. To this point both Berlioz and Liszt pursue the line that was
to be taken by Wagner, absorbed as he was with the heroic figures of the
Nibelungenlied. Later, Sibelius was to follow in their footsteps with his
extensive use of the Finnish epic, the Kalevala.

Structure: Theme and variations. The Score Sketch which follows ends
with Variation II.

Orchestra:

2 Flutes (FL)	2 Horns (HN)
Piccolo (PIC)	2 Trumpets (TR)
2 Oboes (OB)	3 Trombones (TB)
2 Clarinets (CL)	Tuba (TU)
2 Bassoons (BN)	
3 Timpani (TIMP)	Piano Solo (P)
Cymbals (CYM)	Violins (VL 1, 2)
Triangle (TRI)	Violas (VA)
Tamtam	Violoncellos (VC)
	Contrabasses (CB)

164

DIES IRAE

VAR.3 MOLTO VIVACE

FOR DISCUSSION: COMPARISONS

1. Though the Berlioz work is the earlier of the two, its orchestra is considerably larger. Since both works deal with similar subject matter, why is the Liszt orchestra leaner than the Berlioz? Which of the two composers is the more original in orchestration?

2. Both works make effective use of the Dies irae (Day of Wrath) chant from the Catholic Requiem Mass. Yet the two composers' ways of treating this theme differ markedly. What is this difference in treatment? Are there other themes in the Berlioz? In the Liszt?

3. In the Berlioz, at the first entrance of the chant, bells sound in the background. Is there symbolic meaning here?

4. What is the significance of the virtuosic solo piano part in the Totentanz? Does the colloquy between soloist and full orchestra work to heighten or lessen dramatic tension? How does this colloquy compare with those written by other composers working in the same medium? Compare Beethoven's Fifth Piano Concerto, Schumann's A minor Piano Concerto, and Tchaikovsky's First Piano Concerto.

5. The Dies irae is, of course, modal; it is in the Aeolian mode. To what extent do both compositions utilize harmony derived from this modal scale? Where and how is this done?

6. Despite the modal scales and harmony heard in both the Symphonie Fantastique and the Totentanz, the pieces are essentially chromatic. Note the sliding diminished 7th chords in the strings at the beginning of the "Witches' Sabbath" and the several glittering bravura passages using chromatically derived figures in the Liszt work. How does each composer blend and/or juxtapose modal and chromatic sonorities? Does this sonorous harmonic blend imply a contradiction?

LIED, "DEATH AND THE MAIDEN" (1817)

STRING QUARTET, "DEATH AND THE MAIDEN," OP. POSTH. (1824),
SECOND MOVEMENT

Franz Schubert (1797-1828)

With Schubert the concept of song was never distant. The lyric element
saturates his instrumental works: the symphonies, chamber music,
sonatas, and character pieces for piano. In fact, several of Schubert's
finest works, including the Quartet quoted here, were derived from his own
lieder. The "Trout" Quintet and the "Wanderer" Fantasy for piano are
other examples.
     The song "Death and the Maiden," however, does not display the
usual Schubertian "tunefulness." The vocal line, especially in the second
part (m. 22), plays a subsidiary role to the dark harmony of the keyboard
part. It is the chordal color, more than the melody, that illuminates the
meaning of the text. In a sense, the lyricism here is harmonic, not
melodic.

Performance forces:

Song: Contralto voice and piano
String quartet: Violin 1, violin 2, viola, violoncello

Structure of quartet movement: Theme and variations

Chords: Roman and arabic numerals. The roman numeral indicates the
scale degree the chord is built upon. An arabic numeral indicates either
an inverted chord or an extended chord. L (leading tone) indicates the
seventh degree of the scale when it is a minor 2nd below the tonic.

A slash (/) indicates that the chord is chromatic (neighbor dominant
function).

"Death and the Maiden" (Words by Matthias Claudius; translated by Dr. Martin Robbins)

The Maiden:
> Pass by me, O, pass by me,
> Go, skeleton so fierce.
> I am still young, Death, leave me,
> And do not seize me here, and do not seize me here.

Death:
> Give me your hand, you lovely, tender child,
> Your friend, I do not come to harm you.
> Be not afraid, I am not wild;
> You'll sleep so soft when my arms hold you.

(This translation fits the music and can be sung.)

FOR DISCUSSION

1. The musical setting of the maiden's words is starkly contrasted to that of the voice of death. Compare in terms of melody, rhythm, harmony, and register.

2. In the piano introduction (mm. 1–8) and in the portion sung by Death (mm. 22–37), the prevailing mode is minor (D minor), but in the closing piano part the mode changes to major (D major). What is the symbolic value of this final shift into the parallel major?

3. Compare this song with "Erlkönig" (1815) by Schubert, which also grapples with the problem of youth and death. Study the relationship of text to music in both songs.

THEME / G MINOR

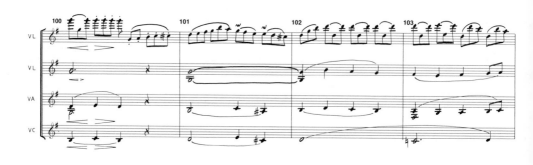

LA REPETIZIONE POCO A POCO
CRESCENDO SINO AL *ff*

FOR DISCUSSION

1. Every structural element in the theme from the second movement of
    the quartet (mm. 1-24) is of a simple nature. Discuss rhythm, melody,
    harmony, and form. Why does this theme's uninvolved character pro-
    vide exceptional compositional opportunities in the variations that
    follow?

2. What is the character of the five variations? Are they of the orna-
    mental type, where the basic contour of the melody is retained in each
    variation, but embroidered? Or are they of the characteristic type,
    where the relation between original melody and variation is more
    subtle? Compare these variations with the variations in the Clarinet
    Quintet by Mozart.

3. Note the dramatic turn of the music in Variation 3. What compositional
    techniques does the composer use here to achieve dramatic excitement?
    With this in mind, how does Schubert manage the change into the more
    relaxed atmosphere of the fourth variation?

4. Discuss the effect and role of the coda beginning at m. 161. Note that
    the theme from the quartet's second movement is related to certain
    portions of the song only: to the piano introduction and to the second
    member of the form (mm. 22-43). Why did Schubert use only these
    portions of the lied? Why did Schubert not use the same key for both
    the lied and the second movement of the quartet?

PART V THE TWENTIETH CENTURY

The one word that best characterizes the trends in twentieth-century music is experimentation. Experimentation in twentieth-century music has led to the use of synthesis and predetermination on a scale that surpassed all previous efforts in this direction.

It began with Debussy. Although a few composers before Debussy had taken some tentative steps, it was he who determinedly and definitely opened the door to experimentation in extensive use of synthesis. The conscious addition or fusion of new elements to normal practices established Debussy as an innovator and led to the ultimate abandonment of tonality.

Debussy's fusing of the pentatonic and the church modes with traditional practices was one step toward the break away from the major-minor tradition. This conscious synthesis was indicative of a new attitude that turned away from the usual evolution or development of a style out of the immediate past. Though Debussy did not himself abandon tonality, he greatly expanded the possibilities of traditional harmonic procedure.

Two ways in which Debussy cleared a path for the abandonment of tonality were his use of the whole tone scale and his use of pandiatonicism. Each of these prepared the way for the use of the twelve-tone row. The synthetic whole-tone scale, in avoiding the characteristic half-steps present in other scales, eliminated the tendencies of melodic tones to move in a particular direction. Each tone is as important as the other in a melodic sense. And this turned out to be one of the distinctive features of the twelve-tone row. Pandiatonicism led in the same direction by its seemingly indiscriminate use of any or all tones (in any order) of a particular mode. Another practice of Debussy was parallel chord movement in which chords were treated as color rather than as part of a traditional chordal progression. Debussy also used the tritone both melodically and harmonically to create vacillation, rather than progression toward a tonal center.

It is interesting to note that Debussy's work did not result in a school or produce a large group of Impressionist composers. Rather, Debussy's music served as a catalyst.

Stravinsky (1882- -) was proclaimed a revolutionary by many people after his Rite of Spring was presented in Paris in 1913. But an examination of the work clearly shows that he was a direct heir to the legacy of Debussy. Stravinsky, in addition to receiving the legacy of Debussy, enlarged upon it and added to it. For example, Stravinsky expanded the principle of parallelism to include polyparallelism. He did the same with the use of the tritone. His chief contribution in the Rite of Spring was a new concept of rhythm: a dynamic, barbaric, explosive rhythm brought about by changing meters overlaid with constantly changing accents.

Debussy's treatment of dissonance as color rather than function opened the way for every experiment with dissonance that was to be made in the twentieth century. Schoenberg, who was ultimately to introduce the concept of the equality of all twelve tones, was also Debussy's heir. He spoke of Debussy's harmonies as "deprived of constructive significance" and serving a coloristic purpose in a new way. "In this way, tonality be-

187

comes already dethroned in practice, if not in theory." Schoenberg was to take the practice and theory of Debussy all the way to "the emancipation of dissonance."

The early works of Arnold Schoenberg (1874-1951) had been in the full Romantic tradition. His symphonic cantata Gurrelieder (1901), a work of huge proportions, was one of his last works in this style; he then turned to a more intimate type of expression, as in his Kammersymphonie (1906) for 15 instruments. Here we find the influence of Debussy, including use of the whole tone scale.

Schoenberg continued to search for his own personal style, going through a period of expressionistic writing, exemplified by Pierrot Lunaire (1912). He had also tried various experiments with non-tonal writing, especially in the Three Piano Pieces, Op. 11 (1908). In 1923, after many years of searching, he arrived at his system of writing with twelve equal tones. The twelve-tone row, in which the order of the tones is predetermined, is a logical consequence of the use of the whole tone scale and other practices of Debussy.

The two chief disciples of Schoenberg in twelve-tone writing, or serial composition, were Anton Webern (1883-1945) and Alban Berg (1885-1935). Both students of Schoenberg, each brought his own personality to the method of writing with twelve tones. Webern's style was concise and compressed, with special emphasis on the use of pointillistic orchestral shadings and textures. At the same time he distilled his musical thoughts into tight, condensed statements which require close attention on the part of the listener. Berg was much more romantic than Webern in his approach to serial writing, and was not willing to abandon all implications of tonality.

As Stravinsky had brought a new dynamic concept of rhythm to twentieth-century music, so too did Bela Bartók (1881-1945). Each was strongly stimulated and influenced by the folk music of his native land: Stravinsky by that of Russia; Bartók, that of Hungary. Although both became exceedingly sophisticated composers, the folk music influences of their heritage served as a constant link to the eternal simplicities.

Bartók, with his compatriot Zoltán Kodály, had gone out into the field to record the authentic folk music of Hungary and other East European countries, ultimately compiling over 2000 items. The rhythmic freedom of many of these folk songs was to have a lasting effect on Bartók's musical style. The six volumes of Bartók's Mikrokosmos for piano are an easily accessible source for study.

Bartók said that Debussy "restored a feeling for chords to all musicians. He was as important as Beethoven who revealed to us progressive form, and as Bach who introduced us to the transcendence of counterpoint. I always ask myself, could one make a synthesis of these three masters and create a vital contemporary style?"

Bartók has been called eclectic because he was influenced by many sources, including Debussy. It might be more accurate to say that Bartók approached each new work as a new problem to solve, a new experiment to try. This attitude is evident in the Mikrokosmos, where the title of the piece is often an indication of the "small world" in which the experiment is to take place: "Major Seconds Broken and Together," "Studies in Double Notes," "Whole-tone Scale" (these titles are all from Volume V).

By mid-century many composers were writing under the influence of Stravinsky, Schoenberg, and Bartók — and, sporadically, the innovations of jazz. The influences of Stravinsky, Bartók, and also Hindemith flourished in the 1940's, but by 1950 it seemed that the strongest influence was to be that of Schoenberg. Many composers hailed Schoenberg's system as the new system: it removed the necessity of constant experimentation and seemed to provide a comfortable, and perhaps foolproof, method once you had mastered it. Both Stravinsky and Bartók had continued to experiment, and Hindemith had delivered his thesis The Craft of Musical Composition, which now started to seem out of date. No one except Schoenberg had evolved a radical new system.

But what of the idea of experiment, of synthesis, of new things? Charles Ives (1874-1954), discovered late, turned out to be one of the most imaginative minds of the twentieth-century musical scene. He anticipated Stravinsky's experiments in polyharmony, the use of mixed and changing time signatures, and the effect of "total sound" as exploited by avant-garde jazz musicians. But Ives's music was discovered late, and therefore his influence was negligible in the first half of the twentieth century.

The idea of experiment by mid-century was not only well-established as an approach to composition, but some experiments were being conducted outside of the main influence which we have discussed. Their impact has been noticeable, but not nearly so influential or far-reaching.

We can mention these tentative experiments only briefly. Henry Cowell (1897-1965), an avowed experimentalist, kept his mind open to all possibilities of new expression. His favorite device, the use of tone clusters, and another, the direct plucking of the piano strings, he passed on to John Cage (1912), who became a strong voice in the encouragement of new experiments. The "prepared" piano was one of Cage's major contributions to twentieth-century performance media. Cage further experimented with the use of silence and of noise. He has also been active in another contemporary activity that interests many composers: random music. Random music may be written in such a way that various sections can be played in any order. Or music may be combined with sounds (musical or otherwise) pre-recorded on tape.

"Aleatory music" is another type of random music. The term comes from the word alea, meaning dice. The aleatory approach to musical composition, in which chance plays a major role, illustrates the attempt in many quarters to get away from the control of the composer and thus eliminate all subjective influence. Of course, the ultimate in doing away with the composer is composition by computer.

Experimentation has traveled a long way since the beginning of the twentieth century. There are those who think the composer may be completely replaced by the computer. If they are right, the computer technician will, of course, take the composer's place.

LA MER (THE SEA), FIRST MOVEMENT

Claude Debussy (1862–1918)

Ten years after L'Après-midi d'un Faune, and shortly after completing his only opera, Pelléas et Mélisande, Debussy turned his energies toward the composition of the three symphonic sketches titled La Mer. Though Debussy uses the cyclic principle in this work, it does not conform to traditional formal structures.

    The first movement, titled "De l'Aube à Midi sur la Mer" ("From Dawn to Noon on the Sea"), presents a succession of themes which are not developed as in former periods, but rather reiterated with changing orchestration. Although drama is not lacking, this is not Debussy's first concern. Rather, Debussy's approach might be called an unfolding of melodic elements suffused with kaleidoscopic orchestral colors.

    La Mer was completed in 1905 when Debussy was at the height of his powers, and it was first performed in Paris at the famous Concerts Lamoureux in October of the same year.

Structure: Free

Orchestra:

2 Flutes (FL)	4 French Horns (HN)
1 Piccolo (PIC)	3 Trumpets (TR)
2 Oboes (OB)	3 Trombones (TB)
1 English Horn (EHN)	1 Tuba (TU)
2 Clarinets (CL)	
2 Bassoons (BN)	
3 Timpani (TIMP)	Violins (VL 1, 2)
Cymbals (CYM)	Violas (VA)
Tamtam	Violoncellos (VC)
2 Harps (HP)	Contrabasses (CB)

ANALYTICAL NOTES

1. The first movement or sketch, "From Dawn to Noon on the Sea," is divided into four sections. The first portion, mm. 1–30, with the key signature of two sharps, serves as an introduction to the next three sections, which are in the keys of D flat major, B flat major, and again D flat major.

    The axis tone (a more accurate term than tonic) of the first 30 measures is the tone B. It serves as a pedal point for 11 measures, and thenceforth is part of a two–note basso ostinato that occurs in 11 of the remaining 21 measures.

    The important theme fragment presented by the trumpet and English horn in mm. 9–17 does not occur again in the first movement, but returns in the third movement where it is extensively treated.

2. The pentatonic basis for the movement that was hinted at in mm. 3–5 becomes fully clear from m. 31 on. Debussy sets the murmuring background in the strings by a pervading use of the notes of the pentatonic scale on D flat. Against this background Debussy presents the horn theme (mm. 35–40) in the Mixolydian mode on D flat. This modal mix (pentatonic and Mixolydian) provides piquant dissonance.

3. Note the bare open 5ths in the flutes and clarinets beginning at m. 33, suggesting Eastern influences. This figure, here a leading idea, also serves as coloristic background to other leading melodic elements.

4. A contrasting theme, sturdy and rhythmic, opens the section in B flat major, beginning at m. 84. Note how the rhythmic jab of the first two notes of this melodic idea is subtly transformed later in the horns at m. 116, and then toward the close in the brass at m. 135.

5. See if you can discover the whole tone cast of mm. 115–131. Contrast the color of this section with the conclusion, beginning at m. 132, where Debussy gradually returns to the pentatonic.

THREE DANCES FROM "L'HISTOIRE DU SOLDAT"

Igor Stravinsky (1882 -)

This unique work, The Soldier's Tale (to be read, played, danced, and mimed), was written in Switzerland in 1918. In this work and others of the same period, Stravinsky turns from the large nineteenth-century orchestra to write for a small group of players.

Stravinsky sought the simplicity of texture that was to be found in the orchestras of the café and the nightclub. In addition, American jazz had by now been heard in Europe (on recordings and in live performances), and this work was one of his first to show Stravinsky's interest in this vital mode of expression.

Structure: Based on dance forms

Orchestra (for the complete work):

Clarinet (CL)

Bassoon (BN)

Cornet

Trombone (TB)

Percussion (PERC)

Violin (VL)

Contrabass (CB)

195

196

WALTZ

RAGTIME

THE CURTAIN FALLS AND THEN RISES AGAIN

FOR DISCUSSION

1. The three dances here have the traditional titles of dances which were very popular throughout the world when L'Histoire du Soldat was written. To what extent has Stravinsky relied on traditional rhythmic procedures? How much has he transformed these three expressions into something new?

2. Compare Stravinsky's use of the dance here with that of Bach in his sarabandes, courantes, gigues, and so on. In addition, compare Stravinsky's treatment with that of Chopin in his waltzes, mazurkas, and other dance forms.

3. Compare the use of instruments in this chamber orchestra with other chamber works in this book: Mozart's Clarinet Quintet and Schubert's "Death and the Maiden" Quartet.

VIOLIN CONCERTO, FIRST MOVEMENT

Alban Berg (1885-1935)

Berg's Violin Concerto was completed in August 1935 and was first performed in April 1936. Berg had been approached in 1934 by Louis Krasner,
an American violinist, to write a concerto. The concerto lay dormant in
Berg's mind until the death of Manon Gropius, the daughter of Mahler's
widow. He then planned the work as a memorial to her. It was Berg's last
completed work.

Structural Plan of First Movement:

Measures

1-10	Introduction: Andante
11-103	Section I: Improvisatory style
104-257	Section II
104-136	Scherzando: Allegretto
137-154	Trio I
155-175	Trio II
176-213	Scherzando (like a waltz)
213-228	Folk song
228-257	Conclusion

Orchestra:

2 Flutes/Piccolo (FL/PIC)

2 Oboes/English Horn (OB/EHN)

1 Alto Saxophone/Clarinet (ALTO SAX/CL)

2 Clarinets (CL)

1 Bass Clarinet (BCL)

2 Bassoons (BN)

1 Contrabassoon (CBN)

4 Timpani (TIMP)

Percussion (PERC)

4 Horns (HN)

2 Trumpets (TP)

2 Trombones (TB)

1 Tuba (TU)

Violins (VL 1, 2)

Violas (VA)

Violoncellos (VC)

Contrabasses (CB)

209

ANALYTICAL NOTES

1. Mm. 1-11 (Introduction): The concerto opens with pyramiding perfect 5ths over a sustained pedal point on B flat. This is the central tone of the work in spite of the fact that the work is conceived in the method of the twelve-tone row. The solo violin imitates this pyramid of intervals in the second measure with G as the basic tone; this tone becomes the second important tone of the work.

2. Mm. 11-18: The twelve-tone row of the concerto is diffuse in mm. 11-14, but is presented clearly in the solo violin in mm. 15-18. The row may be treated in different ways. Among these are inversion, retrograde motion, retrograde inversion, and other contrapuntal devices. Various transpositions may be combined with these techniques. See, for example, the inversion of the row in mm. 24-27. Compare this with the original form of the row in mm. 15-18.

3. Berg also planned the row so that the last four notes mesh with the opening four notes of J. S. Bach's Chorale "Es ist Genug." This chorale is the goal of the work, appearing in the second movement.

4. The first section of this work is in quasi-improvisatory style, perhaps suggesting quiet reflection. The contrasting second section, beginning at m. 104 (Allegretto), is freely based on the traditional dance form with trio. Look at the structural plan of the movement.

    Note the use of 3rds at m. 106; these become ever more prevalent (also inverted as 6ths) until at m. 137 (Trio I) the solo violin embarks upon a lyrical passage which leads toward the suggestion of a Viennese waltz beginning at m. 182.

5. In m. 213 Berg introduces a Carpathian folk song. Consider the possible reasons for the use of popular and folk song elements in this movement as contrasted to the use of the chorale, "Es ist Genug," at the close of the work.

INDEX

ABCDE7987654321